WHAT IS SOCIOLOGY ABOUT?

Key Concepts for Students and Teachers

Hichem Karoui

Global East-West (London)

Copyright © [2024] by Hichem Karoui

Global East-West (London)

All rights reserved.

No portion of this book may be reproduced in any form without written permission from the publisher or author except as permitted by copyright law.

Contents

Introduction to Sociology   1
   References For Further Reading

1. The Origins and Development of Sociology   11

   The Evolution of Sociology: Pioneering Contributions and Interdisciplinary Insights
   The Foundations: Pioneers of Sociological Thought
   Interdisciplinary Crossroads: Sociology's Diverse Influences
   Twentieth-Century Transformations: Expanding Sociological Horizons
   Contemporary Developments: Navigating a Complex Social Landscape
   Conclusion: A Discipline in Constant Evolution
   Key Takeaways
   References For Further Reading

2. The History of Sociology   23
   The Evolution of Sociology: Tracing Its Origins and Key Thinkers

Preliminary Influences on Sociology:
Foundational Thinkers:
Functionalism and Conflict Theory:
The Emergence of Contemporary Sociological Paradigms:
Conclusion:
Summary
References For Further Reading

3. Theoretical Perspectives in Sociology   35
    Sociological Perspectives: An In-Depth Analysis
    Summary
    References For Further Reading

4. Research Methods in Sociology   44
    1. Quantitative Research
    2. Qualitative Research
    3. Mixed Methods
    4. Experimental Research
    5. Comparative Research
    Ethical Considerations
    Conclusion
    Summary
    References For Further Reading

5. Socialization and Identity   58
    Exploring the Multifaceted Nature of Socialization and Its Role in Identity Development
    The Importance of Socialization

Contents

Introduction to Sociology   1
    References For Further Reading

1. The Origins and Development of Sociology   11

    The Evolution of Sociology: Pioneering Contributions and Interdisciplinary Insights
    The Foundations: Pioneers of Sociological Thought
    Interdisciplinary Crossroads: Sociology's Diverse Influences
    Twentieth-Century Transformations: Expanding Sociological Horizons
    Contemporary Developments: Navigating a Complex Social Landscape
    Conclusion: A Discipline in Constant Evolution
    Key Takeaways
    References For Further Reading

2. The History of Sociology   23
    The Evolution of Sociology: Tracing Its Origins and Key Thinkers

Preliminary Influences on Sociology:
Foundational Thinkers:
Functionalism and Conflict Theory:
The Emergence of Contemporary Sociological Paradigms:
Conclusion:
Summary
References For Further Reading

3. Theoretical Perspectives in Sociology   35
    Sociological Perspectives: An In-Depth Analysis
    Summary
    References For Further Reading

4. Research Methods in Sociology   44
    1. Quantitative Research
    2. Qualitative Research
    3. Mixed Methods
    4. Experimental Research
    5. Comparative Research
    Ethical Considerations
    Conclusion
    Summary
    References For Further Reading

5. Socialization and Identity   58
    Exploring the Multifaceted Nature of Socialization and Its Role in Identity Development
    The Importance of Socialization

The Dynamics of Socialization
Summary
References For Further Reading

6. Social Structures and Institutions — 70
   Exploring Social Structures and Institutions in Sociology
   Section 1: Comprehending Social Structures
   Section 2: Varieties and Dynamics of Social Structures
   Section 3: Institutions and Their Functions
   Section 4: Illustrative Examples of Social Institutions
   Section 5: Social Structures and Societal Transformation
   Summary
   References For Further Reading

7. Social Stratification and Inequality — 82
   Exploring the Intricacies of Social Stratification and Inequality
   Comprehending Social Stratification
   Theoretical Frameworks of Social Stratification
   Implications and Consequences
   Summary
   References For Further Reading

8. Culture and Society — 93
   The Interwoven Dynamics of Culture and Society
   Defining Culture
   Cultural Universals: Common Threads Amidst Diversity

Culture, Identity, and Socialization
Summary
References For Further Reading

9. Sociology of Religion   104

    Exploring the Sociology of Religion: Theories, Concepts, and Case Studies

    Theoretical Perspectives
    Research Methods
    Key Concepts
    Case Studies
    Summary
    References For Further Reading

10. Deviance and Crime   117

    Elucidating Deviance
    Theoretical Paradigms of Deviance
    The Societal Construction of Crime
    Societal Responses to Deviance
    Deviance, Crime, and the Catalyst for Social Change
    Conclusion
    Summary

    References For Further Reading

11. Social Change and Social Movements   128

Exploring the Intricate Nexus of Social Change and Social Movements
Understanding Social Change
Types of Social Movements
Summary
References For Further Reading

12. The Future of Sociology — 138
    The Future of Sociology: Navigating Challenges and Opportunities
    Globalization and Transnationalism
    Technology and Society
    Environmental Challenges
    Social Justice and Inequality
    Summary
    References For Further Reading

13. Conclusion: A Reflective Journey Through Sociology — 147
    References For Further Reading

14. Sources and References — 153

Introduction to Sociology

Sociology emerged as an academic discipline in the 19th century, primarily due to the sweeping social upheavals of the Industrial Revolution. This epoch heralded a pronounced transition from agrarian, rural communities to burgeoning urban centers characterized by industrialization, engendering profound societal metamorphoses. In the face of rapid transformation, intellectuals and theorists were impelled to dissect the intricate social dynamics and complexities that surfaced amidst these shifts. Sociology emerged as a distinct and consequential field of inquiry within this milieu.

The genesis of sociology can be traced back to the seminal ideas of pioneering sociological thinkers such as Ibn Khaldun, Auguste Comte, Karl Marx, and Émile Durkheim. Each of these intellectuals made pivotal contributions to the scaffolding of sociological theory, thereby establishing a fertile groundwork for ensuing scholars.

Regarded generally as the progenitor of sociology, although he was preceded by the Arab genius Ibn Khaldun, Auguste Comte coined the term "sociology" in the early 19th century. He postulated that societies could be subjected to scientific investigation, employing methodologies akin to those utilized in the natural sciences. Comte advocated for systematically exploring the social realm, underscoring the imperative of empirical evidence and observation in elucidating and decoding social phenomena. His advocacy for positivism aimed to enshrine sociology as a rigorous, scientific discipline, disentangled from metaphysical and religious dogmas surrounding societal interpretations.

While Comte's intellectual framework provided a nascent approach to societal study, Karl Marx—an influential German philosopher and economist—infused a critical lens into the study of capitalist society. Marx scrutinized the intricate interplay between social strata and the economic architecture of society, positing that capitalism fostered intrinsic social inequities. He argued that the bourgeoisie, or capitalist class, systematically exploited the proletariat, representing the working class. In his magnum opuses, "The Communist Manifesto" and "Capital," Marx dissected capitalism's mechanisms and ramifications on social disparity. He posited that societal conflict, especially that emerging between these two factions, was the pivotal catalyst for transformative societal changes. Thus, Marx's theories became foundational to the branch of sociology identified as conflict theory.

Émile Durkheim, a prominent French sociologist, further advanced the discipline by accentuating the study of social facts and the maintenance of social order. Durkheim contended that societal cohesion stemmed from shared values, normative structures, and collective institutions. His notion of "social integration" illuminated the critical role of communal bonds and collective consciousness in preserving social equilibrium. His groundbreaking research on suicide illustrated how societal elements profoundly affect individual actions and mental well-being. Durkheim posited that social phenomena must be understood within their broader context, transcending mere individual psychology. His focus on social structures and institutional frameworks catalyzed the emergence of structural-functionalism, another pivotal theoretical perspective within sociology.

While Comte, Marx, and Durkheim laid the foundational tenets

of sociological thought, other notable theorists broadened and enriched their ideas. Another eminent German sociologist, Max Weber, accentuated the significance of individual agency, motivations, and cultural contexts in shaping social phenomena. His inquiries into bureaucracy and the Protestant ethic underscored rationalization and religion's profound impacts on societal evolution. Weber elucidated how specific cultural values and convictions influenced economic development and social order, contributing significantly to the emergence of sociological paradigms that foreground culture and individual agency.

George Simmel, a notable figure in German sociology, concentrated on micro-level interactions and the pivotal roles of social group dynamics. Simmel examined social interactions, including cooperation, conflict, and competition, and their ramifications on both individual and group behaviors. He championed the importance of analyzing social interactions as discrete yet significant phenomena, illuminating aspects of societal dynamics that might be overlooked when solely concentrating on structural components. Simmel's work fostered foundational insights into the intricacies of social life, paving the way for the development of symbolic interactionism, a crucial theoretical lens within sociology.

As sociology burgeoned, it increasingly embraced an interdisciplinary approach, drawing on insights from diverse fields such as psychology, anthropology, and economics. This amalgamation of disciplines empowered sociologists to probe various social issues and phenomena. Sociological research has traversed topics including race, gender, globalization, social movements, education, familial structures, crime, and deviance, illuminating the complex interrelations among individuals, groups, and society at large. Employing qualitative and quantitative methodologies, sociology utilizes various research techniques, including surveys, interviews, observational studies, content analyses, and statistical evaluations.

In summation, sociology arose from an imperative to comprehend and scrutinize the societal transformations engendered by the Industrial Revolution. The contributions of early sociological luminaries such as Comte, Marx, Durkheim, Weber, and Simmel have been instrumental in shaping sociological theory and methodology. Their foundational ideas laid the groundwork for various theoretical approaches and research techniques that continue to inform the field of sociology. With its interdisciplinary character and extensive research foci, sociology offers profound insights into the social dynamics, structures, and forces that shape our collective existence, aiding us in navigating the complexities inherent in the social realm.

The discipline of sociology epitomizes an ever-evolving and variegated field that renders invaluable perspectives on the convoluted and layered nature of human society. By undertaking a profound and all-encompassing exploration of the social cosmos—its myriad structures, dynamics, and interpersonal exchanges—sociology seeks to illuminate the complexities inherent in human behavior and its intricate correlations with societal forces. Sociologists endeavor to procure a deep-seated comprehension of the interplay between individuals, collectives, and the broader societal framework through meticulous observation, rigorous analysis, and extensive research methodologies. At the heart of this discipline lies the recognition that our social milieu profoundly shapes our cognitive processes, actions, and belief systems. Sociology posits that we are not mere solitary beings; we exist as integral components of a vast network of social interconnections and institutional frameworks.

These social frameworks traverse multiple realms, such as familial constructs, educational institutions, religious affiliations, governance, and economic systems. Sociologists meticulously scrutinize these structures and institutions to excavate the social patterns, norms, and trends that shape our individual narratives and collective experiences.

A fundamental tenet of sociology entails its unwavering commitment to challenging entrenched myths and misconceptions regarding societal structures and individual behavior. Rather than succumbing to the allure of reductive explanations, which simplisticly attribute social phenomena to biological determinism or individual volition, sociology embarks on a deeper investigation into the foundational social forces at play. It probes how systemic frameworks, cultural paradigms, and historical contexts mold our behaviors, attitudes, and identities. Sociologists strive to elucidate the intricate and subtle elements that influence our everyday existence through the lens of varied societies, cultures, and historical timelines.

Social inequality emerges as a significant concern within sociology. This field critically examines the dissonant distribution of power, resources, and opportunities among distinct social factions. By delving into the intersections of race, class, gender, and other identity markers, sociologists unveil intricate systems of advantage, marginalization, and oppression that perpetuate social inequities. Through diligent analysis and advocacy, sociology enriches our understanding of these pressing issues, informing initiatives aimed at cultivating a more just and equitable societal framework.

In pursuit of its scholarly objectives, sociology deploys an array of theoretical constructs and methodological approaches. Sociological theory acts as a conceptual apparatus for interpreting the social domain, elucidating the reasons behind specific patterns and institutional constructs. To illustrate, functionalism elucidates the interdependence intrinsic to social institutions, underlying their role in maintaining societal equilibrium, whereas conflict theory accentuates the power struggles and discord underlying social change. Symbolic interactionism emphasizes how individuals forge meanings through interaction, employing shared symbols and vernacular. These theoretical paradigms empower sociologists to scrutinize and interpret sociological phenomena from multifaceted perspectives.

In the realm of research methodologies, sociologists implement a diverse arsenal of techniques to gather and analyze social data. Surveys, interviews, participant observation, and statistical assessments are routinely utilized to glean insights into attitudes, behaviors, and social trends. These methodologies enable researchers to discern societal patterns and interrelations, thereby perpetually testing and refining sociological theories. The amalgamation of both quantitative and qualitative methods serves to deepen our grasp of the intricate social phenomena at play.

The study of sociology cultivates critical thinking acumen, fosters empathy, and enhances the capability to navigate a kaleidoscope of perspectives. By interrogating societal quandaries and dilemmas, sociology inspires individuals to question commonly accepted assumptions while envisioning alternative avenues and possibilities.

Ultimately, sociology serves as a catalyst for fostering a profound understanding of varied social identities and experiences, thereby promoting values of tolerance, empathy, and the potential for societal metamorphosis. It equips individuals with the instrumental means to scrutinize social phenomena, interrogate prevailing social norms, and actively pursue societal advancement.

Within this book's pages, our sociology exploration will traverse a wide spectrum of topics. We shall delve into the socialization processes, the intricate tapestry of cultural constructs, the dynamics underlying social interactions, the ramifications of social deviance, and the pervasive impact of institutional structures. Throughout our intellectual expedition, we will analyze the ways in which individuals are shaped by their social contexts, the pivotal influence of culture in sculpting societies, the nuanced interplay of social interactions, and the consequences stemming from deviations from established social norms. Furthermore, we will closely examine the extensive ramifications of key institutions—such as family, education, religion, government, and the economy—on both individual trajectories and collective societal life.

References For Further Reading

1. Appelbaum, R. P. (2017). *The Sociological Imagination*. New York: Political Science Press.

2. Berger, P. L., & Luckmann, T. (1966). *The Social Construction of Reality: A Treatise in the Sociology of Knowledge*. New York: Anchor Books.

3. Blumer, H. (1969). *Symbolic Interactionism: Perspective and Method*. Berkeley: University of California Press.

4. Bryman, A. (2016). *Social Research Methods*. Oxford: Oxford University Press.

5. Bourdieu, P. (1986). *The Forms of Capital*. In: Richardson, J. G. (Ed.), Handbook of Theory and Research for the Sociology of Education. New York: Greenwood Press.

6. Castells, M. (2010). *The Rise of the Network Society*. Cambridge: Wiley-Blackwell.

7. Collins, P. H. (2019). *Intersectionality*. Cambridge: Polity Press.

8. Dahrendorf, R. (1959). *Class and Class Conflict in Industrial Society*. Stanford: Stanford University Press.

9. Denzin, N. K., & Lincoln, Y. S. (2011). *The Sage Handbook of Qualitative Research*. Thousand Oaks, CA: SAGE Publications.

10. Durkheim, É. (1982). *The Rules of Sociological Method*. New York: Free Press.

11. Elias, N. (2000). *The Civilizing Process*. Oxford: Blackwell.

12. Ewick, P., & Silbey, S. S. (1995). *Entwined Empires: The Impact of American and English Law on Society*. Law and Society Review, 29(4), 1057-1076.

13. Giddens, A. (2017). *Sociology*. Cambridge: Polity Press.

14. Goffman, E. (1963). *Stigma: Notes on the Management of Spoiled Identity*. Englewood Cliffs, NJ: Prentice Hall.

15. Kendall, D. (2015). *Sociology in Our Times*. Boston: Cengage Learning.

16. Macionis, J. J. (2016). *Sociology*. Upper Saddle River, NJ: Pearson.

17. Merton, R. K. (1968). *Social Theory and Social Structure*. New York: Free Press.

18. Miller, R. (2017). *Understanding Social Institutions: Structures, Dynamics, and Patterns of Action*. New York: Routledge.

19. Piketty, T. (2014). *Capital in the Twenty-First Century*. Cambridge: Harvard University Press.

20. Parsons, T. (1951). *The Social System*. Glencoe, IL: Free Press.

21. Ritzer, G. (2011). *Sociological Theory*. New York: McGraw-Hill.

22. Ruggiero, V. (2018). *Sociology: Theory, Structure, and Action*. New York: Cambridge University Press.

23. Scott, J. (1990). *A Matter of Record: Documentary Sources in Social Research*. Philadelphia: Temple University Press.

24. Tashakkori, A., & Teddlie, C. (2010). *SAGE Handbook of Mixed Methods in Social & Behavioral Research*. Thousand Oaks, CA: Sage Publications.

25. Wacquant, L. (2004). *Body and Soul: Notebooks of an Apprentice Boxer*. New York: Oxford University Press.

CHAPTER ONE

THE ORIGINS AND DEVELOPMENT OF SOCIOLOGY

The Evolution of Sociology: Pioneering Contributions and Interdisciplinary Insights

THE DISCIPLINE OF SOCIOLOGY has undergone a remarkable metamorphosis since its inception, serving as a testament to the visionary contributions of its pioneers and the dynamic nature of interdisciplinary collaboration. This comprehensive literature review explores the depths of sociology's evolution, investigating the groundbreaking works and concepts that have shaped its trajectory and affirmed its significance within the social sciences.

The Foundations: Pioneers of Sociological Thought

The origins of sociology can be traced back to the innovative minds of early thinkers who laid the cornerstone for this discipline. If Auguste Comte (19th century) is frequently recognized as the "father of sociology," Ibn Khaldun (14th century) is its real progenitor, thanks to his famous Al-Muqaddima.

Ibn Khaldun, an Arab scholar born in Tunisia, is recognized as incontestably the pioneering figure in sociology, predating Auguste Comte by several centuries. His seminal work, "Al-Muqaddima," laid the groundwork for various sociological and historical theories, making significant contributions to the understanding of social structures, cultural evolution, and the cyclical nature of civilizations. In this book, he named the discipline he was going to describe and whose methods he would apply: " the science of civilization and human society." (Ibn Khaldun, 2009; Dhaouadi, 2013).

Foundation of Sociology and Historiography:

- Ibn Khaldun is frequently acknowledged as the "father of sociology" and a foundational figure in historiography, having developed theories on social change, civilization, and the evolution of societies long before Western scholars like Comte (Shahidipak, M. 2020; Abdeljabbar, F. 2014;).

Cyclical Theory of Civilizations:

- Ibn Khaldun introduced a cyclical theory of history, describing the rise and fall of civilizations through distinct phases: primitive, village civilization, and splendor. This theory has been applied to various historical contexts, including Indonesian history (Hardanti, B. 2021; Rahmah, A. 2022).

Empirical and Analytical Approach:

- His work emphasized an empirical and analytical approach to understanding social phenomena, focusing on natural causes and the influence of environmental and economic factors on societal development.

Influence on Modern Sociology and Anthropology:

- Contemporary scholars and anthropologists continue to use Ibn Khaldun's theories to explain social changes, the decay of societies, and the impact of governance and economic relations on civilization.

- Western scholars, including orientalists like Gibb, have acknowledged Ibn Khaldun's contributions, often referring to him as the precursor to modern sociology and historiography (Shahidipak, M. 2020; Rahmah, A. 2022).

- His ideas on social change, the decay of societies, and the role of media in contemporary contexts have been utilized by modern anthropologists and sociologists

Integration of Social, Political, and Economic Components:

- Ibn Khaldun's work is recognized for its comprehensive analysis of socio-cultural phenomena, linking the development of societies to historical, political, and economic factors.

- His theories on the influence of geography and climate on social structures and the dichotomy between urban and rural societies were pioneering for their time (Nofal, F. 2021).

Thus, Ibn Khaldun's contributions to sociology and historiography are profound and far-reaching. His empirical approach, cyclical theory of civilizations, and integration of various social components predate and arguably surpass the foundational work of later Western sociologists like Auguste Comte. His insights continue to influence modern sociological and anthropological thought, solidifying his status as a true progenitor of sociology.

However, Auguste Comte introduced the term "sociology" and championed a scientific approach to comprehending societal phenomena (Comte, 1830). His seminal tome, *Course in Positive Philosophy*, was a guiding beacon, emphasizing the necessity for a systematic and empirical investigation of social structures. Comte's influence continues to resonate, inspiring future sociologists to embrace scientific methodologies in their quest for knowledge.

A vital figure in the establishment of sociology is Émile Durkheim. His emphasis on "social facts" and deep exploration of collective consciousness revolutionized sociological thought (Durkheim, 1893). Through his empirical research techniques and concepts such as anomie—a condition of normlessness and social disintegration—he has imparted a lasting impact on the discipline. Durkheim's focus on social integration and the division of labor remains pivotal in contemporary sociological inquiry.

Max Weber, a contemporary of Durkheim, made significant strides in sociological theory, particularly through his distinctive perspective on social action. Weber contended that comprehending social phenomena necessitates an understanding from the actor's perspective, introducing the concept of "Verstehen," or interpretive understanding (Weber, 1922). His work challenged the hegemony of structural functionalism and paved the way for new avenues of sociological inquiry, particularly in the realms of religion, bureaucracy, and social transformation.

Interdisciplinary Crossroads: Sociology's Diverse Influences

Sociology's quintessential characteristic is its inherently interdisciplinary nature. The field draws upon and contributes to an expansive array of disciplines, including philosophy, economics, psychology, and anthropology, among others. This section explores the influential works and concepts that have significantly shaped sociology through these interdisciplinary connections.

The philosophical and economic insights of Karl Marx have had a profound effect on sociological thought. His analysis of class struggle and capitalism, delineated in *The Communist Manifesto* (Marx & Engels, 1848), provided a critical framework for comprehending social inequality and power dynamics. Marx's materialist conception of history, which asserts that the material conditions of society shape its cultural and ideological superstructure, remains a central tenet in sociological discourse.

Psychology's impact on sociology is also notable, especially through the works of Sigmund Freud. Freud's pioneering theories on psychoanalysis and the significance of dreams have yielded invaluable insights into the unconscious mind and its influence on human behavior (Freud, 1920). His innovations have enriched our understanding of social behavior, particularly regarding personality, motivation, and interpersonal interactions.

Twentieth-Century Transformations: Expanding Sociological Horizons

The 20th century heralded a period of rapid growth and specialization within the realm of sociology. This epoch produced influential theorists who developed comprehensive frameworks and methodologies that continue to shape the discipline.

Talcott Parsons, referred to as the "father of modern sociology," made notable contributions with his AGIL paradigm (Parsons, 1951). This theoretical framework—Adaptation, Goal Attainment, Integration, and Latency—offered a systematic approach to understanding social systems and their integration. Parsons' groundbreaking work has significantly influenced sociological theory and methodology, shaping how sociologists conceptualize and investigate social phenomena.

C. Wright Mills, another prominent sociologist of the 20th century, introduced the notion of the "sociological imagination" (Mills, 1959). Mills emphasized that sociologists should connect individual experiences with larger social structures and historical contexts. This perspective has proven instrumental in elucidating the interplay between personal troubles and public issues, urging scholars to consider the broader social and political forces that shape individual lives.

Contemporary Developments: Navigating a Complex Social Landscape

In recent decades, sociology has continued to adapt, evolving in response to the ever-changing social landscape while embracing new methodologies and perspectives. This section analyzes some of the pivotal developments and contributions that have influenced contemporary sociological thought.

Pierre Bourdieu's exploration of cultural capital and social reproduction has been immensely influential in deciphering the mechanics of social inequality (Bourdieu, 1977). His concepts, such as habitus and field, furnish a framework for analyzing how social structures and cultural practices perpetuate social hierarchies. Bourdieu's scholarship has played a crucial role in studies of education, class, and power dynamics.

The advent of feminist sociology has injected a critical perspective into the discipline, challenging traditional frameworks and illuminating gender inequalities. Scholars such as Patricia Hill Collins and Kimberlé Crenshaw have significantly advanced our understanding of intersectionality and the complex fabric of social identities (Collins, 1990). Their work underscores the necessity of considering multiple axes of identity—such as race, class, and gender—in sociological analyses.

Conclusion: A Discipline in Constant Evolution

Sociology's evolution represents a vibrant and ongoing journey, driven by the visionary contributions of its pioneers and the discipline's ability to engage with diverse interdisciplinary perspectives. From the foundational works of Comte, Durkheim, and Weber to recent advancements in theoretical frameworks and methodological approaches, sociology has asserted itself as an essential and influential field within the social sciences.

As sociology continues to advance, it remains vital to reflect on its rich history, engage with varied theoretical orientations, and embrace the interdisciplinary character that has rendered it a powerful tool for understanding the complexities of the social world. The trajectory of sociology is a testament to human curiosity and the relentless pursuit of knowledge, ensuring that its evolution will invariably inform our comprehension of society for generations to come.

***

Key Takeaways

- Sociology as a theory was conceptually framed by Ibn Khaldun, who was the first scholar to describe its main rules and put them into practice in his seminal work in Arabic: Prolegomena (Al-Muqaddima).

- Sociology's evolution is marked by the contributions of pioneers like Comte, Durkheim, and Weber, who established its foundational concepts and methodologies.

- The discipline is inherently interdisciplinary, drawing upon philosophy, economics, psychology, and anthropology.

- Key figures like Marx and Freud significantly influenced sociological thought, contributing frameworks for understanding social inequality and human behavior.

- 20th-century developments, including Parsons' AGIL paradigm and Mills' sociological imagination, shaped contemporary sociological perspectives.

- Contemporary sociology incorporates perspectives like Bourdieu's analysis of cultural capital and feminist critiques emphasizing intersectionality.

- We also emphasized sociology's ongoing evolution, its adaptability to the changing social landscape, and its continued relevance in understanding social complexities.

***

QUESTIONS FOR FURTHER THOUGHT

1. Compare and contrast the sociological perspectives of Auguste Comte, Émile Durkheim, and Max Weber. What are their key contributions, and how do their approaches to understanding society differ?

2. Explain the concept of "social facts" as defined by Durkheim and provide an example of a social fact in contemporary society.

3. Discuss Max Weber's concept of "Verstehen" and its significance for sociological research. How does it differ from a purely positivist approach?

4. Analyze the influence of Karl Marx's ideas on the development of sociology. How has his concept of class struggle shaped sociological perspectives on inequality?

5. Explain the impact of Sigmund Freud's psychoanalytic theories on sociological understanding of human behavior. Provide specific examples.

6. Describe Talcott Parsons' AGIL paradigm and its significance for understanding social systems.

7. What is C. Wright Mills' "sociological imagination," and how does it help us understand the relationship between personal troubles and public issues? Provide an example.

8. Explain Pierre Bourdieu's concepts of "habitus" and "cultural capital" and their relevance to understanding social

inequality and reproduction.

9. Discuss the contributions of feminist sociology and the concept of intersectionality to the field. How have these perspectives challenged traditional sociological approaches?

10. How has the interdisciplinary nature of sociology shaped its evolution and its ability to understand complex social phenomena? Provide examples of disciplines that have influenced sociology.

References For Further Reading

1. Ibn Khaldun, Abderrahman (2009) Al-Muqaddima, Dar Sadir, Beirut, second edition.

2. Bourdieu, P. (1977). Cultural reproduction and social reproduction. In J. Karabel & A. H. Halsey (Eds.), Power and ideology in education (pp. 487-510). Oxford University Press.

3. Collins, P. H. (1990). Black feminist thought: Knowledge, consciousness, and the politics of empowerment. Routledge.

4. Comte, A. (1830). Course in positive philosophy. http://www.gutenberg.org/files/37717/37717-h/37717-h.htm

5. Durkheim, É. (1893). The division of labor in society. Free Press.

6. Freud, S. (1920). Beyond the pleasure principle. https://www.gutenberg.org/files/49417/49417-h/49417-h.htm

7. Marx, K., & Engels, F. (1848). The communist manifesto. https://www.marxists.org/archive/marx/works/1848/communist-manifesto/

8. Mills, C. W. (1959). The sociological imagination. Oxford University Press.

9. Parsons, T. (1951). The social system. Free Press.

10. Weber, M. (1922). The sociology of reli-

gion. https://www.marxists.org/reference/archive/weber/works/sociology/

11. Shahidipak, M. (2020). Ibn Khaldun as a paradigm for the past and future of sociology and humanity. *Sociology International Journal.* https://doi.org/10.15406/sij.2020.04.00240.

12. Abdeljabbar, F.(October 01, 2014). = ☐☐☐☐☐ ☐☐☐Ibn Khaldun / Syed Farid Alatas. Idafat: Arab Journal of Sociology☐ 2014 Issue 28, pp.147-149☐ 2014 Issue 28, pp. 147-149☐ 1.

13. Nofal, F. (2021). "Philosophical robinsonade" of Ibn al-Nafis. *Philosophy Journal.* https://doi.org/10.21146/2072-0726-2021-14-4-98-112.

14. Dhaouadi, Mahmoud. (2013). Ibn Khaldoun : Le Printemps Arabe des Sciences Sociales et Humaines. Dirasat: Human and Social Sciences, Vol.40 Issue 1, pp.174-183, 2013 Vol.40 Issue 1, pp.174-183, 1.

15. Hardanti, B. (2021). TIGA FASE SEJARAH BERDASARKAN PEMIKIRAN IBNU KHALDUN DALAM SEJARAH INDONESIA. *Historiography.* https://doi.org/10.17977/um081v1i22021p178-192

16. Rahmah, A. (2022). PEMIKIRAN SOSIAL BUDAYA IBN KHALDUN. *JOURNAL SCIENTIFIC OF MANDALIKA (JSM) e-ISSN 2745-5955 | p-ISSN 2809-0543.* https://doi.org/10.36312/10.36312/vol3iss4pp271-279.

Chapter Two

The History of Sociology

The Evolution of Sociology: Tracing Its Origins and Key Thinkers

Sociology is a vibrant and continually evolving discipline dedicated to unraveling the intricate tapestry of human behavior and societal constructs. This discourse embarks on a profound exploration of sociology's inception and progressive trajectory, illuminating seminal thinkers, pivotal theories, and the invaluable contributions of preeminent sociologists throughout history.

Preliminary Influences on Sociology:

Ibn Khaldun: A Foundational Influence on Sociological Thought

Before sociology was formally acknowledged as a distinct academic discipline, various intellectuals laid the groundwork for its emergence, among whom Ibn Khaldun stands prominent. This literature review elucidates his remarkable contributions to the social sciences and his enduring influence on the development of sociology.

Ibn Khaldun, a 14th-century Muslim scholar and historian, is widely regarded as a trailblazer in the field of social sciences. His magnum opus, *Muqaddimah* (often referred to as *Prolegomena*), presents a comprehensive analysis of human society and its underlying dynamics, offering insights that continue to inform contemporary sociological inquiry (Ibn Khaldun, 1958).

One of the fundamental aspects of Ibn Khaldun's legacy is his assertion that studying society constitutes a unique domain of scholarly inquiry. He championed the importance of dissecting social structures, cultural norms, and the interactions among diverse social groups (Ibn Khaldun, 1967). This integrative perspective established a foundational framework for what would later be recognized as the sociological imagination, as articulated by C. Wright Mills (Mills, 1959).

Central to Ibn Khaldun's sociological theory is his notion of "Asabiyyah," commonly interpreted as "social cohesion" or "group feeling." He contended that a sense of collective identity and solidarity drives human societies, fundamentally influencing their political, economic, and cultural frameworks (Ibn Khaldun, 1958). This concept has been instrumental in shaping the understanding of social group formation and evolution, subsequently impacting modern sociological theories concerning social cohesion and collective action (Tilly, 1978).

The *Muqaddimah* further elucidates early notions of social change and the progression of history. Ibn Khaldun introduced a cyclical theory of history, positing that societies undergo repetitive patterns of rise and decline. This conception of history, emphasizing the inevitable fluctuations of civilizations, has significantly influenced sociological theories regarding social evolution and historical sociology (Ibn Khaldun, 1958; Wallerstein, 1974).

Moreover, Ibn Khaldun's exploration of social institutions and their ramifications for human behavior constitutes another cornerstone of his work. He meticulously analyzed the influence of governance, religion, and economic frameworks on societal structures, thus anticipating key areas of modern sociological inquiry (Ibn Khaldun, 1969). His insights into the interplay between social institutions and individual actions have notably contributed to developing sociological theories focused on social control and social order (Durkheim, 1893).

Additionally, Ibn Khaldun's methodology holds historical significance, laying the groundwork for subsequent sociological research techniques. His emphasis on empirical observation and systematic data collection for understanding social phenomena foreshadowed modern sociological methodologies (Ibn Khaldun, 1958). His approach, which combines historical analysis with empirical study, has indelibly shaped the field of sociology.

In conclusion, Ibn Khaldun's contributions to the discipline of sociology are both profound and extensive. His holistic examination of society and insights into social cohesion, historical cycles, and social institutions have significantly influenced sociological thought. Scholars recognize his work as a pivotal bridge connecting ancient philosophical traditions with modern social sciences, thereby solidifying his position as a foundational figure in the development of sociology (Hourani, 1983). Through the lens of Ibn Khaldun, we are better equipped to understand the intricate dynamics of societies both past and present, demonstrating his remarkable foresight and intellectual depth.

Then comes Auguste Comte, in the early 19th century. He coined the term "sociology," fervently advocating for the empirical investigation of social phenomena (Comte, 1830). His positivist approach underscored the necessity for a scientific methodology to scrutinize the underpinnings of social order and advancement (Comte, 1851).

Simultaneously, thinkers such as Alexis de Tocqueville grappled with fundamental inquiries regarding societal structures. Through his incisive analysis of American democracy, Tocqueville elucidated the nuances of individualism and its ramifications for social cohesion (Tocqueville, 1835). His observations of the interplay between self-interest and robust local communities in the United States led him to affirm that such dynamics fostered a thriving democratic environment (Tocqueville, 1835).

Furthermore, Harriet Martineau, frequently celebrated as the inaugural female sociologist, approached social issues through a feminist lens (Martineau, 1837). Her seminal work, *Society in America*, proffered profound insights into gender inequality's intricacies and championed calls for societal reforms (Martineau, 1837). Martineau underscored the imperative of viewing social life through the experiences of those marginalized by prevailing social hierarchies (Martineau, 1837).

Foundational Thinkers:

The 19th and early 20th centuries heralded the emergence of influential sociological thinkers whose intellect significantly sculpted the discipline. Karl Marx, among the most profound contributors to sociology and economics, scrutinized capitalist society's structural dynamics, illuminating the perpetual class struggles and exploitative relations therein (Marx, 1848). He posited that capitalism entrenched social disparities, advocating for revolutionary societal metamorphosis (Marx, 1867).

Similarly, Émile Durkheim contributed substantially to the study of social integration and cohesive bonds (Durkheim, 1893). Through his pioneering investigations into suicide, Durkheim elucidated the intricate relationship between collective social factors and individual actions, accentuating the necessity of social solidarity in preserving societal equilibrium and averting the anomie—a condition marked by normlessness and alienation which can permeate modern civilizations (Durkheim, 1897).

Max Weber, revered for his holistic approach to social theory, examined the interplay of religion, bureaucratic governance, and rationalization within the societal framework (Weber, 1904). His exposition of the "Protestant Ethic" delineated the connection between religious convictions and the evolution of capitalist economies while also emphasizing the subjective meanings individuals ascribe to their actions (Weber, 1904). Weber's insistence on contextualizing individual behavior within broader social constructs remains a cornerstone of sociological inquiry (Weber, 1922).

Functionalism and Conflict Theory:

The mid-20th century witnessed the ascent of functionalism and conflict theory as dominant paradigms within sociology. Functionalist theorists, including Talcott Parsons and Robert Merton, conceptualized society as an intricate web of interconnected social institutions (Parsons, 1951; Merton, 1968). Their focus lay in elucidating how these institutions collaborate to sustain social order and stability, illuminating their roles in fostering a harmonious societal existence (Parsons, 1951; Merton, 1968).

Conversely, conflict theory, championed by Karl Marx and further advanced by scholars such as Ralf Dahrendorf, redirected scholarly attention to issues of social inequality and power dynamics (Marx,

1848; Dahrendorf, 1959). Proponents of this perspective underscored the salience of social conflicts as catalysts for transformative change, postulating that societal frameworks often perpetuate the interests of hegemonic groups while deepening systemic inequalities (Marx, 1848; Dahrendorf, 1959). This theoretical orientation highlights the critical importance of power structures, class disparities, and social stratifications in sculpting social interactions (Marx, 1848; Dahrendorf, 1959).

The Emergence of Contemporary Sociological Paradigms:

In recent decades, sociology has burgeoned into a multifaceted discipline, boasting an array of contemporary perspectives reflective of the evolving social landscape. Symbolic interactionism, as advocated by sociologists like George Herbert Mead and Erving Goffman, delineates how individuals imbue symbols with meanings and interact with one another, thus shaping their social realities (Mead, 1934; Goffman, 1959). This paradigm underscores the significance of micro-level interactions in forming broader societal structures (Mead, 1934; Goffman, 1959).

Feminist theory foregrounds the centrality of gender in deciphering power relations, subjugation, and social progression (Collins, 1990). Feminist sociologists critically assess patriarchal systems and ardently argue for incorporating women's experiences and viewpoints within sociological analyses (Collins, 1990). The concept of intersectionality plays a pivotal role in this discourse, illuminating the intricate interrelations among varied dimensions of social inequity, such as race, class, and sexuality (Crenshaw, 1989).

Postmodernism, as a theoretical lens, disrupts traditional sociological assumptions and methodologies (Lyotard, 1979). Proponents of this approach contend that social reality is inherently complex and multifaceted, emphasizing the fluidity of identity, the pervasive influence of language and discourse, and the paramount significance of subjective experiences (Lyotard, 1979). Postmodern sociology aims to interrogate grand narratives, ultimately deconstructing established social constructs and fostering a more nuanced comprehension of social phenomena (Lyotard, 1979).

Conclusion:

The historical trajectory of sociology reveals it as a dynamic discipline, perpetually adapting in response to an ever-shifting social milieu. From its nascent inquiries into social phenomena to the influential contributions of key sociological thinkers across various epochs, sociology remains at the forefront of elucidating the myriad complexities inherent in human behavior and social systems. Through an in-depth exploration of sociology's rich historical fabric, we glean invaluable insights into the theoretical frameworks and perspectives that have shaped the discipline and continue to enrich our understanding of contemporary society. These diverse outlooks coalesce to provide a holistic comprehension of the social world, informing initiatives geared towards ameliorating social issues and advocating for social equity.

**

Summary

We traced the evolution of sociology, highlighting key thinkers like

Ibn Khaldun, Auguste Comte, and others. We explored foundational theories such as functionalism and conflict theory and examined contemporary perspectives, including feminist and postmodern approaches.

Key takeaways

* We explored sociology's historical development, beginning with early influences like Ibn Khaldun and his concept of "Asabiyyah."

* Key figures in the development of sociology include Auguste Comte (coining the term), Harriet Martineau (early feminist perspective), Karl Marx (conflict theory), Émile Durkheim (social integration), and Max Weber (holistic approach).

* Dominant sociological paradigms discussed include functionalism (Parsons, Merton), conflict theory (Marx, Dahrendorf), symbolic interactionism (Mead, Goffman), feminist theory, and postmodernism.

* Ibn Khaldun's contributions to social sciences, including his cyclical history theory and analysis of social institutions, significantly impacted sociological thought.

***

QUESTIONS FOR FURTHER THOUGHT

1. Compare and contrast Ibn Khaldun's concept of "Asabiyyah" with Durkheim's ideas on social solidarity. How do these concepts relate to social cohesion and the maintenance of social order?

2. Explain the contributions of Auguste Comte to the de-

velopment of sociology, highlighting his approach and its limitations.

3. Discuss the differing perspectives of Karl Marx and Émile Durkheim on the nature of society and social change. How do their theories reflect different views on social order and conflict?

4. Analyze Harriet Martineau's contribution to sociology, emphasizing her unique perspective and its significance for the field. How did her work challenge existing sociological paradigms?

5. Describe the core tenets of functionalism and conflict theory. Provide examples of how these theoretical perspectives explain social phenomena.

6. Explain Max Weber's concept of "verstehen" (understanding) and its importance in sociological research. How does it relate to his analysis of the Protestant ethic and the spirit of capitalism?

7. Discuss the emergence of contemporary sociological paradigms such as symbolic interactionism, feminist theory, and postmodernism. How do these approaches differ from earlier theoretical perspectives?

8. Analyze the role of intersectionality in feminist theory and its significance for understanding social inequality.

9. Evaluate the impact of Ibn Khaldun's work on the development of sociological thought, considering his methodological approaches and theoretical contributions.

10. How does the text demonstrate sociology's evolution as a dynamic and adaptable discipline responsive to societal

changes? What are some of the ongoing challenges and debates within the field?

velopment of sociology, highlighting his approach and its limitations.

3. Discuss the differing perspectives of Karl Marx and Émile Durkheim on the nature of society and social change. How do their theories reflect different views on social order and conflict?

4. Analyze Harriet Martineau's contribution to sociology, emphasizing her unique perspective and its significance for the field. How did her work challenge existing sociological paradigms?

5. Describe the core tenets of functionalism and conflict theory. Provide examples of how these theoretical perspectives explain social phenomena.

6. Explain Max Weber's concept of "verstehen" (understanding) and its importance in sociological research. How does it relate to his analysis of the Protestant ethic and the spirit of capitalism?

7. Discuss the emergence of contemporary sociological paradigms such as symbolic interactionism, feminist theory, and postmodernism. How do these approaches differ from earlier theoretical perspectives?

8. Analyze the role of intersectionality in feminist theory and its significance for understanding social inequality.

9. Evaluate the impact of Ibn Khaldun's work on the development of sociological thought, considering his methodological approaches and theoretical contributions.

10. How does the text demonstrate sociology's evolution as a dynamic and adaptable discipline responsive to societal

changes? What are some of the ongoing challenges and debates within the field?

References For Further Reading

1. Durkheim, É. (1893). *The division of labor in society*. Free Press.

2. Hourani, G. F. (1983). *Arab seafarers: Ibn Khaldun's interpretation of the evidence*. International Journal of Middle East Studies, 15(2), 159-176.

3. Ibn Khaldun. (1958). *The Muqaddimah: An introduction to history*. (F. Rosenthal, Trans.). Princeton University Press.

4. Ibn Khaldun. (1967). *The Muqaddimah: New interpretations of history*. (N. J. Dawood, Trans.). Routledge & Kegan Paul.

5. Ibn Khaldun. (1969). *The Mediterranean in the 14th century: North Africa, Syria, and Egypt*. (S. Khoury, Trans.). Saqi Books.

6. Mills, C. W. (1959). *The sociological imagination*. Oxford University Press.

7. Tilly, C. (1978). *From mobilization to revolution*. Addison-Wesley.

8. Wallerstein, I. (1974). *The modern world-system: Capitalist agriculture and the origins of the European world-economy in the sixteenth century*. Academic Press.

9. Comte, A. (1830). A general view of positivism.

10. Comte, A. (1851). The positive philosophy of Auguste

Comte.

11. Dahrendorf, R. (1959). Class and class conflict in industrial society. Stanford University Press.

12. Durkheim, É. (1893). The division of labor in society. Free Press.

13. Durkheim, É. (1897). Suicide: A study in sociology. Free Press.

14. Goffman, E. (1959). The presentation of self in everyday life. Anchor Books.

15. Marx, K. (1848). The communist manifesto.

16. Marx, K. (1867). Capital: Critique of Political Economy.

17. Mead, G. H. (1934). Mind, self, and society: From the standpoint of a social behaviorist. University of Chicago Press.

18. Merton, R. K. (1968). Social theory and social structure. Free Press.

19. Parsons, T. (1951). The social system. Free Press.

20. Tocqueville, A. de. (1835). Democracy in America.

21. Weber, M. (1904). The Protestant ethic and the spirit of capitalism.

22. Weber, M. (1922). Economy and society: An outline of interpretive sociology.

Chapter Three

Theoretical Perspectives in Sociology

Sociological Perspectives: An In-Depth Analysis

Sociology, as a nuanced discipline (Durkheim, 1895; Marx, 1848; Mead, 1934), endeavors to probe the intricate tapestry of human behavior and interpersonal dynamics. To facilitate this exploration, sociologists employ a plethora of theoretical frameworks that provide diverse vantage points for analyzing societal structures and interactions. These theoretical lenses elucidate the fabric of society, elucidate the interplay of individuals and collectives, and illuminate the mechanisms of social transformation (Durkheim, 1895; Marx, 1848; Mead, 1934).

In this discourse, we shall traverse three seminal theoretical frameworks within sociology: functionalism (Durkheim, 1895), conflict theory (Marx, 1848), and symbolic interactionism (Mead, 1934). Each framework proffers its own distinct perspective on societal organization, inherent discord, and the subjective interpretations ascribed by individuals to their social encounters.

Functionalism, often referred to as structural functionalism (Durkheim, 1895), conceptualizes society as an intricate system comprised of interrelated components that collaboratively foster social cohesion and stability. Advocates of this perspective draw parallels between society and a biological organism (Durkheim, 1895), positing that various institutions and social structures fulfill essential roles to maintain the overall functionality of the societal whole. Proponents assert that institutions—such as the family, educational systems, and religious entities—serve pivotal roles in sustaining social equilibrium and addressing the requisite functions of society (Durkheim, 1895). Emile Durkheim, frequently hailed as the progenitor of sociology (Durkheim, 1895), accentuated the interdependence of social institutions and their critical contribution to fulfilling societal needs.

To further dissect functionalism, we can scrutinize its foundational concepts. A quintessential notion is social integration (Durkheim, 1895), which denotes the extent to which individuals within a society perceive themselves as interconnected and possess a sense of belonging. Functionalists contend that elevated levels of social integration bolster societal stability and cohesion (Durkheim, 1895), believing that institutions like family and education are integral to nurturing these connections by imparting values, norms, and socialization processes.

In addition, the concept of social differentiation (Durkheim, 1895) merits attention. Social differentiation pertains to the specialization and division of labor within a societal framework (Durkheim, 1895). Functionalists argue that this division is paramount for efficiently addressing societal needs and ensuring the seamless operation of various institutional functions (Durkheim, 1895). Individuals are allocated roles and responsibilities in alignment with their competencies and qualifications, fostering a harmonious and industrious society.

Transitioning to conflict theory—an ideology primarily propagated by Karl Marx (Marx, 1848)—this perspective zeroes in on social inequality and the contestation for power and resources endemic to societal constructs (Marx, 1848). Conflict theorists maintain that society is inherently characterized by perpetual strife and rivalry among diverse social factions (Marx, 1848), informed primarily by disparities in wealth, authority, and social prestige. They assert that institutional frameworks perpetuate systemic inequalities (Marx, 1848), with dominant groups striving to preserve their hegemony over resources.

An exploration of conflict theory necessitates an examination of its central tenets. One paramount concept is social class (Marx, 1848), which delineates the hierarchical stratification present in society relative to individuals' access to resources and their positionality within the economic continuum (Marx, 1848). Conflict theorists assert that social class constitutes a significant driver of social inequality (Marx, 1848), with power disparities between classes shaping societal structures. They draw attention to the role of capitalism in engendering and perpetuating these inequalities (Marx, 1848), as capitalists endeavor to maximize profits while laborers advocate for equitable wages and improved working conditions.

Moreover, social stratification—another pivotal construct of conflict theory (Marx, 1848)—refers to the classification of society into disparate layers predicated on parameters like income, occupation, and education (Marx, 1848). Conflict theorists argue that such stratification is not an outcome of individual merit but rather a mechanism through which elites consolidate control and uphold their privileged standing (Marx, 1848). This view elucidates the incessant struggle amongst divergent groups for social resources and the manner in which inequalities are legitimized and fortified through prevailing ideologies and institutional practices (Marx, 1848).

Symbolic interactionism, a further dominant theoretical paradigm (Mead, 1934), underscores the subjective significances individuals ascribe to their social interactions (Mead, 1934). Proponents of this perspective argue that society is actively constructed through the continual process of individuals interpreting symbols and engaging in direct interactions (Mead, 1934). They emphasize the crucial role of both linguistic and non-linguistic symbols, gestures, and shared significances in shaping social realities and identities (Mead, 1934).

To delve deeper into symbolic interactionism, one may consider its essential concepts. The notion of the self is particularly salient (Mead, 1934), referring to an individual's conception of identity and existence within the societal framework (Mead, 1934). Symbolic interactionists assert that the self is not a static entity but rather evolves through social engagements and the meanings individuals attach to those interactions (Mead, 1934). Central to this notion is Cooley's concept of the "looking-glass self," which posits that individuals cultivate their self-concept based on perceived perceptions from others (Cooley, 1902).

Another vital concept within this paradigm is socialization (Mead, 1934)—the enduring process through which individuals assimilate and internalize the norms, values, and behaviors characteristic of their society (Mead, 1934). Symbolic interactionists contend that socialization transcends a mere transmission of information, occurring instead through dynamic communication that enables individuals to negotiate and reinterpret collective meanings within their social spheres (Mead, 1934). This iterative process facilitates identity formation, social role acquisition, and participation in the co-construction of social reality (Mead, 1934).

While these theoretical paradigms each present valuable insights into sociological inquiry, they are not mutually exclusive (Durkheim, 1895; Marx, 1848; Mead, 1934). Sociologists frequently adopt a synergistic approach, amalgamating elements from these theories to grasp the intricacies of social phenomena holistically (Durkheim, 1895; Marx, 1848; Mead, 1934). For instance, functionalism addresses societal stability (Durkheim,

1895), while conflict theory accentuates power dynamics and social disparities (Marx, 1848). Concurrently, symbolic interactionism elucidates the subjective lived experiences and meanings individuals attribute to their interactions within these expansive social frameworks (Mead, 1934).

Beyond functionalism, conflict theory, and symbolic interactionism, other pivotal theoretical lenses merit consideration. Feminist theory, for instance, scrutinizes the role of gender in shaping social life and investigates how power relations between genders influence societal structures and individual lived experiences (Collins, 1990). Postmodernism critiques the notion of a singular, objective reality, focusing instead on the fragmentation and multiplicity of experiences and the influence of language and discourse on social constructivism (Lyotard, 1984). Furthermore, rational choice theory, drawing on economic principles, applies calculations of rational decision-making to social interactions and institutions, elucidating how individuals navigate choices based on perceived costs and benefits (Becker, 1962).

In summation, sociological theoretical frameworks serve as instrumental tools for dissecting the multifaceted and complex nature of society (Durkheim, 1895; Marx, 1848; Mead, 1934). By engaging with these perspectives, sociologists unveil the patterns, structures, and processes that mold individuals, collectives, and societal norms. This nuanced understanding enables a critical examination of social phenomena, the identification of latent inequalities and conflicts, and the envisioning of avenues for transformative social change (Durkheim, 1895; Marx, 1848; Mead, 1934).

***

Summary

We explored three major sociological perspectives—functionalism, conflict theory, and symbolic interactionism—detailing their core tenets and key thinkers (Durkheim, Marx, Mead). We briefly mentioned other relevant theories like feminist theory and postmodernism.

Key Takeaways

- We introduced and analyzed three major sociological perspectives: functionalism (Durkheim), conflict theory (Marx), and symbolic interactionism (Mead).

- Functionalism views society as an interconnected system where institutions maintain stability and social cohesion.

- Conflict theory emphasizes social inequality, power struggles, and resource competition among different social groups.

- Symbolic interactionism focuses on how individuals interpret and create meaning through social interactions and symbols.

- Key concepts within each perspective are defined and discussed, such as social integration and differentiation (functionalism), social class and stratification (conflict theory), and the self and socialization (symbolic interactionism).

- We highlighted that these perspectives are not mutually exclusive and can be combined to achieve a more holistic understanding of society.

- Additional sociological theories like feminist theory, postmodernism, and rational choice theory are briefly introduced.

***

QUESTIONS FOR FURTHER THOUGHT

1. Explain Durkheim's concept of social integration and its role in maintaining social order according to functionalism.

2. Describe Marx's concept of social class and its relationship to social inequality within conflict theory.

3. How does symbolic interactionism differ from both functionalism and conflict theory in its approach to understanding social phenomena?

4. Explain Mead's concept of the "self" and its development through social interaction. Include Cooley's "looking-glass self" in your answer.

5. Define socialization within the context of symbolic interactionism and discuss its importance in shaping individual identity.

6. What is social stratification, and how do functionalist and

conflict theorists explain its existence?

7. Discuss the concept of social differentiation as explained by Durkheim.

8. How can sociological theories be used in a complementary rather than mutually exclusive way? Provide examples.

9. Briefly describe feminist theory, postmodernism, and rational choice theory and how they contribute to sociological understanding.

***

References For Further Reading

1. Becker, G. S. (1962). Irrational Behavior in Economic Theory. Southern Economic Journal, 29(2), 113-122.

2. Collins, P. H. (1990). Black Feminist Thought: Knowledge, Consciousness, and the Politics of Empowerment. Routledge.

3. Cooley, C. H. (1902). Human Nature and the Social Order. Scribner's.

4. Durkheim, E. (1895). The Rules of Sociological Method. Free Press.

5. Lyotard, J.-F. (1984). The Postmodern Condition: A Report on Knowledge. University of Minnesota Press.

6. Marx, K. (1848). The Communist Manifesto. Penguin

Classics.

7. Mead, G. H. (1934). Mind, Self, and Society: From the Standpoint of a Social Behaviorist. University of Chicago Press.

Chapter Four

Research Methods in Sociology

In sociology, research methodologies stand as foundational pillars that underpin the investigation and comprehension of the multifaceted social phenomena that shape human existence (Babbie, 2021). These methods are meticulously crafted to collect and analyze data systematically, aiming to yield profound insights and expand our knowledge of the social sphere. This chapter endeavors to elucidate the diverse research techniques employed in sociology, accentuating their respective advantages, limitations, and ethical implications.

1. Quantitative Research

Quantitative research in sociology entails aggregating and analyzing numerical data to uncover social patterns, relationships, and trends (Creswell, 2014). This approach utilizes statistical techniques to measure and scrutinize data gathered through surveys, questionnaires, or preexisting datasets. By incorporating extensive sample sizes, quantitative research aspires to deliver generalized conclusions that hold relevance for larger populations.

Strengths:

Classics.

7. Mead, G. H. (1934). Mind, Self, and Society: From the Standpoint of a Social Behaviorist. University of Chicago Press.

Chapter Four

Research Methods in Sociology

In sociology, research methodologies stand as foundational pillars that underpin the investigation and comprehension of the multifaceted social phenomena that shape human existence (Babbie, 2021). These methods are meticulously crafted to collect and analyze data systematically, aiming to yield profound insights and expand our knowledge of the social sphere. This chapter endeavors to elucidate the diverse research techniques employed in sociology, accentuating their respective advantages, limitations, and ethical implications.

1. Quantitative Research

Quantitative research in sociology entails aggregating and analyzing numerical data to uncover social patterns, relationships, and trends (Creswell, 2014). This approach utilizes statistical techniques to measure and scrutinize data gathered through surveys, questionnaires, or preexisting datasets. By incorporating extensive sample sizes, quantitative research aspires to deliver generalized conclusions that hold relevance for larger populations.

Strengths:

- Furnishes precise numerical data conducive to statistical analysis, facilitating exact measurements and comparisons (Bryman, 2016).

- Empowers researchers to test hypotheses and delineate cause-and-effect relationships (Field, 2013).

- Tends to be more objective than qualitative methods, thereby mitigating researcher bias (Robson & McCartan, 2016).

Limitations:

- Quantitative techniques may oversimplify complex social phenomena, sidelining the subjective experiences and meanings associated with them (Hammersley, 2013).

- Restricted in capturing the nuances of social interactions and the contextual elements influencing human behavior (Denzin & Lincoln, 2011).

- An over-reliance on numerical data may obscure significant qualitative dimensions of social life (Tashakkori & Teddlie, 2010).

2. Qualitative Research

Qualitative research investigates the subjective experiences, significances, and interpretations that individuals associate with social phenomena (Patton, 2015). This methodology encompasses in-depth interviews, participant observation, and comprehensive analyses of documents or texts. Through qualitative research, sociologists gain intricate insights into social interactions, cultural practices, and the complexities inherent in human behavior (Silverman, 2016).

Strengths:

- Provides rich, nuanced descriptions and explanations of social phenomena (Mason, 2018).

- Facilitates the exploration of underlying meanings, social processes, and personal experiences (Charmaz, 2014).

- Allows for examining dynamic and context-sensitive social phenomena (Flick, 2018).

Limitations:

- Findings may lack generalizability owing to smaller sample sizes and the highly contextual nature of qualitative research (Wengraf, 2001).

- Susceptibility to researcher bias during data collection and analysis (Cohen, Manion, & Morrison, 2017).

- Time-consuming and resource-intensive, often limiting the viability of large-scale studies (Creswell & Poth, 2017).

Qualitative research encompasses several pivotal methodologies:

- **a) In-depth interviews:** Researchers conduct open-ended discussions with individuals or small groups to elicit rich qualitative data, exploring participants' perspectives, experiences, and interpretations of social phenomena (Kvale & Brinkmann, 2015).

- **b) Participant observation:** Researchers immerse themselves in the social environments they examine, actively observing and engaging in social activities. This method provides a more nuanced comprehension of social behaviors and interactions (DeWalt & DeWalt, 2010).

- **c) Content analysis:** Researchers systematically analyze written, visual, or auditory materials to discern themes, patterns, and meanings. By scrutinizing texts such as literature, news articles, or social media content, they can glean insights into cultural norms, social discourses, and ideological influences (Neuendorf, 2017).

3. Mixed Methods

Mixed methods research synergistically merges elements of both quantitative and qualitative approaches, aspiring to deliver a comprehensive analysis of social issues (Tashakkori & Teddlie, 2010). This technique generally involves an initial phase of quantitative data collection and analysis, subsequently followed by the integration of qualitative methods to enrich the understanding of the topic.

Strengths:

- Facilitates a holistic exploration of intricate social phenomena by incorporating both numerical and qualitative data (Johnson & Onwuegbuzie, 2004).

- It strengthens the credibility and validity of findings by triangulating and convergent diverse data sources (Patton, 2015).

- Affords an opportunity to approach research questions from multiple perspectives (Creswell, 2014).

Limitations:

- Engaging in mixed-methods research can be labor-intensive and resource-heavy (Rocco, Bliss, Gallagher, & Perez-Prado, 2003).

- Requires proficiency in both quantitative and qualitative research methodologies (Fetters, Curry, & Creswell, 2013).

- The intricate integration of data poses challenges, necessitating potential trade-offs between depth and breadth of analysis (Guetterman, Fetters, & Creswell, 2015).

4. Experimental Research

Experimental research systematically manipulates variables to elucidate cause-and-effect relationships within social phenomena (Campbell & Stanley, 1966). This methodology establishes controlled settings replicating real-world situations to test specific hypotheses. While this approach provides robust internal validity in establishing causation, generalizing findings to broader populations in naturalistic settings can be challenging (Shadish, Cook, & Campbell, 2002).

Strengths:

- Creates a controlled environment for researchers to manipulate variables and establish causal links (Cook & Campbell, 1979).

- Ensures high internal validity by minimizing confounding variables (Maxfield & Babbie, 2009).

- Permits the replication of experiments to verify the robustness of findings (Salkind, 2010).

Limitations:

- Artificial constructs may not fully encapsulate the complexities of real-world situations (McCoy, 2012).

- Ethical dilemmas may arise from deliberately manipulating or controlling variables (Zimbardo, 2007).

- Extrapolating findings to real-life contexts is challenging due to the contrived nature of experimental environments (Yin, 2018).

5. Comparative Research

Comparative research aims to scrutinize and juxtapose social phenomena across various societies, cultures, or groups (Wimmer & Gallo, 2013). This approach enables sociologists to investigate the effects of distinct social, political, and economic factors on human behavior and social institutions. It provides insights into both the commonalities and divergences among societies, illuminating universal patterns and particularities.

Strengths:

- Enables the identification of similarities and differences across distinct societies, cultures, or historical periods (Simmons, 2015).

- Enhances understanding of how social phenomena are shaped by unique sociocultural contexts (Mahoney & Thelen, 2015).

- Facilitates the recognition of global patterns and processes (Ragin & Amato, 1994).

Limitations:

- May neglect the specific historical, political, and cultural nuances that characterize individual societies (King, Keohane, & Verba, 1994).

- Ensuring comparability between varied societies or cultures can be challenging due to differing contexts and operational definitions (Przeworski & Teune, 1970).

- Heavily reliant on existing data sources, which can introduce bias and constrain the scope of research (Beck, 2005).

Ethical Considerations

Adherence to ethical standards is paramount in conducting sociological research. Researchers must secure informed consent from participants, ensuring that they comprehend the research objectives, methodology, potential risks, and benefits (Beauchamp & Childress, 2013). Safeguarding confidentiality and privacy is essential, along with ensuring anonymity whenever feasible (American Sociological Association, 2017). Additionally, researchers are obliged to minimize harm, promote the well-being of participants, and respect their autonomy as informed individuals (Liamputtong, 2007).

Conclusion

Research methodologies in sociology are pivotal to enhancing our comprehension of the social landscape. Sociologists can unveil invaluable insights into social behaviors, structures, and transformations using quantitative, qualitative, mixed methods, experimental, and comparative approaches. Adhering to ethical principles serves as a guiding framework to protect participants and uphold the integrity of research findings. Through rigorous and principled research methods, sociology fosters a more informed and equitable society by elucidating the complexities of human social existence (Giddens, 2013).

***

Summary

We have detailed various sociological research methodologies, including quantitative, qualitative, mixed methods, experimental, and comparative approaches, outlining their strengths, limitations, and ethical considerations.

Key Takeaways

- Sociology utilizes diverse research methods to understand social phenomena.

- Quantitative research uses numerical data for statistical analysis, offering precision but potentially oversimplifying complexities.

- Qualitative research explores subjective experiences and meanings, providing rich insights but potentially lacking generalizability.

- Mixed methods combine quantitative and qualitative approaches for comprehensive analysis.

- Experimental research manipulates variables to establish causality in controlled settings, but generalizability can be limited.

- Comparative research analyzes social phenomena across different societies, revealing similarities and differences.

- Ethical considerations, including informed consent and minimizing harm, are crucial in all sociological research.

***

QUESTIONS FOR FURTHER THOUGHT

1. Define quantitative research in sociology and provide two strengths and two limitations of this approach.

2. What are the three main qualitative research methodologies described in the text, and briefly explain each one?

3. What is mixed methods research, and what are its key strengths and limitations?

4. Explain the principles of experimental research in sociology, including its strengths and limitations.

5. Describe the goals of comparative research and identify two strengths and two limitations of this approach.

6. According to the text, what are the ethical considerations that sociologists must address when conducting research?

7. Compare and contrast quantitative and qualitative re-

search methods in terms of their focus, data collection techniques, and types of insights they provide.

8. Why is it important for sociological research to adhere to ethical standards?

9. Based on the text, what are the overall goals of sociological research, and how do different methodologies contribute to achieving these goals?

10. Choose one research method discussed (e.g., quantitative, qualitative, mixed methods, experimental, comparative) and explain a potential research question that could be effectively addressed using that method, justifying your choice.

References For Further Reading

1. American Sociological Association. (2017). *Code of Ethics*.

2. Babbie, E. (2021). *The Basics of Social Research*. Cengage Learning.

3. Beauchamp, T. L., & Childress, J. F. (2013). *Principles of Biomedical Ethics*. Oxford University Press.

4. Beck, U. (2005). *Power in the Global Age*. Polity Press.

5. Bryman, A. (2016). *Social Research Methods*. Oxford University Press.

6. Campbell, D. T., & Stanley, J. C. (1966). *Experimental and Quasi-Experimental Designs for Research*. Houghton Mifflin.

7. Charmaz, K. (2014). *Constructing Grounded Theory*. SAGE Publications.

8. Cohen, L., Manion, L., & Morrison, K. (2017). *Research Methods in Education*. Routledge.

9. Cook, T. D., & Campbell, D. T. (1979). *Quasi-Experimentation: Design & Analysis Issues for Field Settings*. Houghton Mifflin.

10. Creswell, J. W. (2014). *Research Design: Qualitative, Quantitative, and Mixed Methods Approaches*. SAGE Publications.

11. Creswell, J. W., & Poth, C. N. (2017). *Qualitative Inquiry and Research Design: Choosing Among Five Approaches*. SAGE Publications.

12. DeWalt, K. M., & DeWalt, B. R. (2010). *Participant Observation: A Guide for Researchers*. Rowman & Littlefield.

13. Denzin, N. K., & Lincoln, Y. S. (2011). *The SAGE Handbook of Qualitative Research*. SAGE Publications.

14. Fetters, M. D., Curry, L. A., & Creswell, J. W. (2013). *Achieving Integration in Mixed Methods Designs—Principles and Practices*. Health Services Research, 48(6), 2134-2156.

15. Field, A. (2013). *Discovering Statistics Using IBM SPSS Statistics*. SAGE Publications.

16. Flick, U. (2018). *An Introduction to Qualitative Research*. SAGE Publications.

17. Giddens, A. (2013). *Sociology*. Polity Press.

18. Guetterman, T. C., Fetters, M. D., & Creswell, J. W. (2015). *Integrating Qualitative and Quantitative Methods in Social Research*. SAGE Research Methods.

19. Hammersley, M. (2013). *What Is Qualitative Research?* Continuum.

20. Johnson, R. B., & Onwuegbuzie, A. J. (2004). *Mixed Methods Research: A Research Paradigm Whose Time Has Come*. Educational Researcher, 33(7), 14-26.

21. King, G., Keohane, R. O., & Verba, S. (1994). *Designing Social Inquiry: Scientific Inference in Qualitative Re-*

search. Princeton University Press.

22. Kvale, S., & Brinkmann, S. (2015). *InterViews: Learning the Craft of Qualitative Research Interviewing*. SAGE Publications.

23. Liamputtong, P. (2007). *Researching the Vulnerable: A Guide to Sensitive Research Methods*. SAGE Publications.

24. Mahoney, J., & Thelen, K. (2015). *Advances in Comparative-Historical Analysis*. Cambridge University Press.

25. Mason, J. (2018). *Qualitative Researching*. SAGE Publications.

26. Maxfield, M. G., & Babbie, E. (2009). *Research Methods for Criminal Justice and Criminology*. Wadsworth Cengage Learning.

27. Neuendorf, K. A. (2017). *The Content Analysis Guidebook*. SAGE Publications.

28. Patton, M. Q. (2015). *Qualitative Research & Evaluation Methods*. SAGE Publications.

29. Przeworski, A., & Teune, H. (1970). *Quantitative Methodology in Comparative Politics*. Random House.

30. Ragin, C. C., & Amato, F. (1994). *Constructing Social Research: The Unity and Diversity of Method*. Pine Forge Press.

31. Robson, C., & McCartan, K. (2016). *Real World Research*. Wiley.

32. Rocco, T. S., Bliss, L., Gallagher, D. J., & Perez-Prado, A. (2003). *Taking the Next Step: Mixed Methods Re-*

search in Organizational Systems. Information Technology, Learning, and Performance Journal, 21(1), 19-26.

33. Shadish, W. R., Cook, T. D., & Campbell, D. T. (2002). *Experimental and Quasi-Experimental Designs for Generalized Causal Inference*. Houghton Mifflin.

34. Silverman, D. (2016). *Doing Qualitative Research*. SAGE Publications.

35. Simmons, A. (2015). *Comparative Social Research: Theoretical and Methodological Issues*. Emerald Group Publishing.

36. Salkind, N. J. (2010). *Encyclopedia of Research Design*. SAGE Publications.

37. Tashakkori, A., & Teddlie, C. (2010). *Mixed Methodology: Combining Qualitative and Quantitative Approaches*. SAGE Publications.

38. Wengraf, T. (2001). *Qualitative Research Interviewing: Biographic Narrative and Semi-Structured Methods*. SAGE Publications.

39. Wimmer, A., & Gallo, J. (2013). *A Guide to Comparative Research*. Social Forces, 91(3), 775-802.

40. Yin, R. K. (2018). *Case Study Research and Applications: Design and Methods*. SAGE Publications.

41. Zimbardo, P. G. (2007). *The Lucifer Effect: Understanding How Good People Turn Evil*. Random House.

Chapter Five

Socialization and Identity

Exploring the Multifaceted Nature of Socialization and Its Role in Identity Development

In this discourse, we shall explore the intricate and nuanced process of socialization and its significant influence on the evolution of individual identity. Socialization represents a lifelong odyssey wherein individuals assimilate the norms, values, beliefs, and behavioral paradigms intrinsic to their society, thereby forging their self-concept within that milieu (Mead, 1934; Giddens, 2017). The ensuing discussion aims to investigate the profound implications of socialization, scrutinize its myriad agents, and furnish a robust understanding of how socialization serves to mold our identities.

The Importance of Socialization

Socialization stands as a cornerstone of human existence, as it metamorphoses individuals into effective constituents of society. Through the prism of socialization, we gather the requisite knowledge and competencies to adeptly navigate and engage with our social surroundings (Berk, 2018). Socialization cultivates a collective consciousness by imparting societal norms and values, engendering stability within the social order. Without socialization, individuals would face considerable challenges in comprehending the expectations and behaviors vital for effective participation in societal life (Durkheim, 1897).

Furthermore, socialization is not a phenomenon confined to the early years of life but a continuous process that endures throughout one's lifespan. Our socialization processes adapt and metamorphose as we traverse new social landscapes and experiences. By acknowledging the essential nature of socialization and its enduring character, we can better understand the intricacies of human behavior and the dynamics of social interaction (Erikson, 1968).

Agents of Socialization

Numerous agents contribute to the socialization process, each playing a distinct role in forming our identities. These agents encompass families, educational institutions, peer groups, media, and religious organizations (Henslin, 2013). Let us delve into the significance of each element, elucidating their influence on our journey of socialization:

1. **The Family**: Serving as the foremost and most pivotal agent of socialization, the family shapes the nascent stages of individual development (Papalia & Martorell, 2015). Children assimilate language, values, norms, and behaviors specific to their cultural or societal construct through their interactions with parents and primary caregivers. The intricacies of family dynamics, parenting methodologies, and the perpetuation of cultural legacies profoundly shape the dialectic of socialization. As children observe and emulate behaviors manifested within their familial context, they gradually internalize the values and

norms, which become integral to their emerging identities (Rosenberg, 2014).

2. **The Educational System**: Functioning as a formalized institution of socialization, the educational system plays a crucial role in the cultivation of individuals (Coleman, 1961). Beyond imparting academic knowledge and skills, schools facilitate the socialization of children into the broader fabric of societal expectations. Pupils acquire not just subject-specific insights but also critical social skills—such as cooperation, teamwork, and deference to authority. The educational environment is a conduit for students to grasp and assimilate societal norms, values, and cultural practices. Additionally, education catalyzes social mobility, empowering individuals to transcend the confines of their circumstantial limitations (Bourdieu, 1986).

3. **Peer Groups**: Peer groups emerge as significant players in the socialization process, particularly during the tumultuous years of adolescence (Brown & Larson, 2009). As young people forge friendships and engage with peers, they acquire essential social competencies, navigate conflicts, and refine their identities through shared experiences. Peer affiliations provide a reservoir of support, acceptance, and opportunities for learning as individuals interact with those who share analogous experiences. Such engagements expose individuals to a spectrum of perspectives and cultural influences, facilitating the ongoing evolution of their identities (Youniss & Yates, 1997).

4. **Media**: The media—comprising various forms such as television, cinema, advertising, and digital platforms—has ascended as a formidable agent of socializa-

tion. Media profoundly influences our beliefs, attitudes, and worldviews, sculpting our comprehension of acceptable and normative behaviors (Thompson, 1995). Furthermore, it plays a pivotal role in shaping perceptions regarding race, gender, and various dimensions of identity. The portrayals within media contribute to the construction and perpetuation of societal stereotypes, wielding considerable power over the development of individual identities (Hall, 1997).

5. **Religious Institutions**: Religious entities represent another vital agent of socialization, offering moral direction, ceremonial practices, and a profound sense of purpose (Chaves, 2011). They significantly shape individuals' spiritual identities and ethical frameworks. The beliefs and rituals espoused by these institutions often serve as a moral compass, guiding our discernment of right and wrong. Moreover, religious institutions foster community and belonging, promoting social cohesion and facilitating identity formation (Smith, 2003).

The Dynamics of Socialization

Socialization encompasses a perpetual process that begins at birth and endures throughout the human experience (Buss, 2020). It involves acquiring and internalizing societal norms, values, and anticipations. This process can be delineated into two primary phases: primary and secondary socialization.

1. **Primary Socialization**: During early childhood's formative years, primary socialization is predominantly influenced by parents or primary caregivers (Miller, 2011). At this juncture, children cultivate fundamental language

skills and assimilate the core concepts of their culture. Through observation and imitation of surrounding behaviors, children internalize the values and norms exhibited by familial figures. This initial phase lays the groundwork upon which individuals construct their identities.

2. **Secondary Socialization**: This phase transpires through interactions with other significant institutions and individuals beyond the familial sphere (Furstenberg, 2000). As individuals mature, their socialization broadens to encompass teachers, friends, mentors, and colleagues. Such interactions impart additional knowledge and skills, guiding individuals toward effective societal participation. Secondary socialization facilitates the acquisition of specific roles, responsibilities, and identities pertinent to chosen vocations, social circles, or professional personas. This process enhances the multifarious character of human identities.

Gender Socialization

A critical dimension of the socialization process is gender socialization, which examines how individuals learn the expectations, behaviors, and roles assigned according to their gender (Lorber, 1994). From the moment of birth, societal structures and familial dynamics allocate roles and expectations predicated on a child's sex. Parents may unwittingly select gendered toys, attire, and activities, reinforcing established gender stereotypes. Children absorb gender-specific behaviors, values, and philosophies throughout their formative years through familial interactions, peer relationships, media influence, and broader societal imprints (Ruble et al., 2007).

Comprehending the ramifications of gender socialization is imperative for recognizing and addressing gender disparities and stereotypes. By investigating the construction and reinforcement of gender roles, society can endeavor to forge more egalitarian systems nurturing diverse and inclusive gender identities (Messner, 2000).

The Essence of Identity Formation

Socialization is instrumental in forming identity, contributing to our self-perception and relational dynamics with others (Erikson, 1968). Identity encompasses a plethora of dimensions, including race, ethnicity, social class, religion, and sexuality. These dimensions are not discrete; rather, they intersect and interplay, shaping our self-concept and sense of belonging (Crenshaw, 1989). The process of identity formation is dynamic, evolving over time as individuals navigate various social contexts and encounters.

Moreover, our sense of identity is intricately linked to our self-concept and self-esteem (Baumeister, 1998). Self-concept refers to our cognitive understanding of ourselves, imbued with our beliefs, perceptions, and values. In contrast, self-esteem entails the appraisal of our intrinsic worth and value as individuals. The experiences of socialization and the feedback garnered from the community substantially influence the development of both self-concept and self-esteem (Rosenberg, 1965).

Conclusion

Socialization is an enduring journey that intricately molds individuals into societal members, sculpting their thoughts, attitudes, and behaviors. Through diverse agents of socialization, individuals assimilate the norms, values, and anticipations that underpin their identities. By recognizing the crucial significance of socialization and its influence on identity formation, we can glean deeper insights into human behavior and the complexities of societal dynamics.

Additionally, understanding the various socialization agents—such as family, education, peers, media, and religious institutions—provides valuable perspectives on how socialization affects individuals differently according to their sociocultural contexts. By critically examining these processes, society can strive toward creating a more just and inclusive world that celebrates the rich diversity of human identities and lived experiences.

***

Summary

We explored the multifaceted process of socialization, its agents (family, education, peers, media, religion), its impact on identity formation, and its ongoing nature throughout life.

Key Takeaways

- Socialization is a lifelong process of assimilating societal norms and values, shaping individual identity.

- Family, education, peer groups, media, and religious institutions are key agents of socialization, each playing a distinct role.

- Primary socialization occurs in early childhood, primarily through family, while secondary socialization continues throughout life through various institutions and interactions.

- Gender socialization significantly influences identity development through societal expectations and learned behaviors.

- Identity formation is a dynamic process influenced by socialization experiences, leading to self-concept and self-esteem development.

- Understanding socialization is crucial for comprehending human behavior and societal dynamics.

- Examining socialization processes can lead to a more just and inclusive society.

***

QUESTIONS FOR FURTHER THOUGHT

1. Define socialization and explain its importance in human development.

2. Identify and describe at least five agents of socialization, explaining their respective roles in shaping an individual's identity.

3. Distinguish between primary and secondary socialization, providing examples of each.

4. Explain the concept of gender socialization and its impact on developing gender roles and identities.

5. How do family dynamics influence the socialization process?

6. Discuss the role of the educational system in socializing children beyond academic learning.

7. How does media influence the formation of individual identities and societal perceptions?

8. What is the relationship between socialization, self-concept, and self-esteem?

9. Explain how religious institutions contribute to socialization and identity formation.

10. Critically analyze the statement: "Socialization is a lifelong process." Explain your reasoning using examples from the text.

References For Further Reading

1. Baumeister, R. F. (1998). The Self. In D. T. Gilbert, S. T. Fiske, & G. Lindzey (Eds.), *The Handbook of Social Psychology* (Vol. 1, pp. 680-740). McGraw-Hill.

2. Berk, L. E. (2018). *Development Through the Lifespan* (7th ed.). Pearson.

3. Bourdieu, P. (1986). The Forms of Capital. In J. Richardson (Ed.), *Handbook of Theory and Research for the Sociology of Education* (pp. 241-258). Greenwood Press.

4. Brown, B. B., & Larson, J. (2009). Peer Relationships in Adolescence. In W. F. Overton (Ed.), *Developmental Psychology: Vol. 2. Theoretical models of human development* (pp. 740-804). Wiley.

5. Buss, D. M. (2020). Evolutionary Psychology: The New Science of the Mind (6th ed.). Routledge.

6. Chaves, M. (2011). The Future of American Religious Diversity. *The Forum*, 9(1), Article 5.

7. Coleman, J. S. (1961). *The Adolescent Society: The Social Life of the Teenager and Its Impact on Education*. Free Press.

8. Crenshaw, K. (1989). Demarginalizing the Intersection of Race and Sex: A Black Feminist Critique of Antidiscrimination Doctrine, Feminist Theory and Antiracist Politics. *University of Chicago Legal Forum*, 1989(1), 139-167.

9. Durkheim, E. (1897). *Le Suicide*. Presses Universitaires de

France.

10. Erikson, E. H. (1968). *Identity: Youth and Crisis*. W.W. Norton & Company.

11. Furstenberg, F. F. (2000). The sociology of adolescent development. In W. Damon & R. M. Lerner (Eds.), *Handbook of Child Psychology* (Vol. 1, pp. 95-139). John Wiley & Sons, Inc.

12. Giddens, A. (2017). *Sociology* (8th ed.). Polity Press.

13. Hall, S. (1997). Representation: Cultural Representations and Signifying Practices. In S. Hall (Ed.), *Representation: Cultural Representations and Signifying Practices* (pp. 1-12). SAGE Publications Ltd.

14. Henslin, J. M. (2013). *Sociology: A Down-to-Earth Approach* (10th ed.). Pearson Education.

15. Lorber, J. (1994). Night to His Day: The Social Construction of Gender. In P. M. J. Ferree, J. Lorber, & R. J. Smith (Eds.), *Revisioning Gender* (pp. 57-67). Sage Publications.

16. Mead, G. H. (1934). *Mind, Self, and Society*. University of Chicago Press.

17. Messner, M. A. (2000). "Barbie Girls vs. Sea Monsters": Children Constructing Gender. *Sociological Forum*, 15(2), 221-233.

18. Miller, P. H. (2011). *Theories of Childhood: An Introduction to Dewey, Montessori, Erikson, Piaget, and Vygotsky*. Palgrave Macmillan.

19. Papalia, D. E., & Martorell, G. (2015). *Experience Human Development* (14th ed.). McGraw-Hill.

20. Rosenberg, M. (1965). *Society and the Adolescent Self-Image*. Princeton University Press.

21. Rosenberg, M. (2014). *The Self-Concept: Theory and Research*. In R. J. Sternberg & K. Sternberg (Eds.), *Cognitive Psychology* (6th ed., pp. 425-444). Cengage Learning.

22. Ruble, D. N., Martin, C. L., & Berenbaum, S. A. (2007). Gender Development. In W. Damon & R. M. Lerner (Eds.), *Handbook of Child Psychology* (6th ed., Vol. 3, pp. 858-932). John Wiley & Sons.

23. Smith, C. (2003). *American Evangelicalism: Embattled and Thriving*. University of Chicago Press.

24. Thompson, J. B. (1995). *The Media and Modernity: A Social Theory of the Media*. Stanford University Press.

25. Youniss, J., & Yates, M. (1997). *Community Service and Social Responsibility in Youth*. Chicago University Press.

Chapter Six

Social Structures and Institutions

Exploring Social Structures and Institutions in Sociology

IN THIS CHAPTER, WE will explore social structures and institutions in sociology in depth. Social structures encapsulate the intricate patterns of relationships and interactions extant within a societal framework, while institutions embody the entrenched norms, values, and practices that delineate and influence social conduct (Giddens, 1993). Acquiring a nuanced understanding of social structures and institutions provides profound insights into the foundational organizational tenets that shape human behavior and the overarching contours of our social milieu (Bourdieu, 1986).

Section 1: Comprehending Social Structures

1.1 Elucidating Social Structures:

Social structures represent complex, multifaceted frameworks that govern the modalities of interaction and relational dynamics among individuals within a society (Durkheim, 1984). These structures transcend mere external variables; they are profoundly embedded in individual consciousness, shaping identities, roles, and comportments (Giddens, 1984).

1.2 Constituents of Social Structures:

To attain a comprehensive grasp of social structures, it is imperative to scrutinize the various constituents that contribute to their genesis. These constituents include social roles, which encompass the expectations and behavioral patterns linked to specific statuses or positions (Turner, 2010); social status, indicative of an individual's relative rank within the societal hierarchy; social groups, which signify collectives of individuals united by common purposes or interests (Simmel, 1971); and social networks, the intricate webs of interconnections and relationships amongst individuals (Wasserman & Faust, 1994).

Section 2: Varieties and Dynamics of Social Structures

2.1 Formal Social Structures:

Formal social structures are explicit, often rigid systems that society establishes to fulfill particular functions (Eisenstadt, 1964). Exemplars of such structures include governmental entities, legal frameworks, educational institutions, and economic organizations, all characterized by predefined roles, regulations, and hierarchical arrangements. These structures confer societal stability and order while regulating power dynamics and resource allocation (Weber, 1978).

2.2 Informal Social Structures:

Conversely, informal social structures emerge organically from individuals' quotidian interactions and relationships (Geertz, 1973). They are typified by implicit rules, social norms, and shared understandings prevalent within social groups and networks. Informal structures significantly influence social customs, behaviors, and traditions. Case studies of informal social structures encompass friendship networks, cultural communities, and social movements (Granovetter, 1973).

Section 3: Institutions and Their Functions

3.1 Defining Institutions:

Institutions constitute the substrate of social existence, forming the collective frameworks and systems through which society organizes itself (North, 1990). They propagate a set of norms, values, regulations, and practices that orchestrate social interactions and fulfill designated functions. Institutions are entrenched and wield substantial influence over individual beliefs, behaviors, and decisions (Scott, 1995).

3.2 Institutional Functions:

Institutions fulfill many societal functions, often interlinked and mutually reliant (Coleman, 1990). Primarily, they establish regulation and social order by defining boundaries, instituting rules, and providing mechanisms for conflict resolution (Searle, 1995). This infrastructure engenders a sense of predictability and stability, facilitating navigation through the social milieu. Secondly, institutions are pivotal in socialization, embedding individuals within shared cultural norms, values, and behaviors (Parsons, 1951). This continuity fosters societal stability by transmitting generations' knowledge, skills, and social expectations. Finally, institutions are instrumental in resource distribution, allocating material resources, opportunities, and rewards among diverse social collectives (Giddens, 2000).

Section 4: Illustrative Examples of Social Institutions

4.1 The Family as an Institution:

The family is a fundamental institution prevalent in all societies, serving as the primary unit for socialization, procreation, and emotional sustenance (Furstenberg, 2000). Families impart cultural values, shape social identities, and influence individual beliefs and actions (Bott, 1971). Familial structures exhibit cultural variability, ranging from nuclear to extended family configurations or alternative kinship networks, with differing societal norms governing these relationships that evolve over time.

4.2 Education as an Institution:

Educational institutions function as vital catalysts for socialization and the dissemination of knowledge (Bowles & Gintis, 1976). They prepare individuals for adult life's multifaceted responsibilities and challenges, providing formal education and equipping them with requisite skills essential for social and economic engagement. Moreover, education serves as a conduit for social mobility, empowering individuals to transcend their initial social standings through acquiring knowledge (Lucas, 2001). The role of educational institutions is intricately shaped by societal aspirations, cultural values, and economic imperatives, manifesting in diverse educational systems globally (Slaughter & Rhoades, 2004).

4.3 Economic Institutions:

Economic institutions encapsulate the systems and frameworks through which societies produce, distribute, and consume goods and services (North, 1990). They mold economic relationships, forge employment opportunities, and influence the distribution of wealth and resources within a society. Economic institutions can manifest in various forms—be they traditional, capitalist, or socialist systems—each engendering distinct patterns of economic organization and behavior (Piketty, 2014). The forces of globalization and technological innovation perpetually reshape these institutions, challenging established paradigms and engendering new opportunities alongside inequalities (Stiglitz, 2012).

4.4 Political Institutions:

Political institutions regulate the processes and frameworks through which societies undertake collective decision-making, allocate power, and enforce laws (Lasswell, 1950). They encompass governmental structures, legal systems, political parties, and other components integral to executing political power. Political institutions are paramount for sustaining social order, safeguarding citizens' rights, and providing avenues for democratic participation and governance (Mair, 2006). These institutions evolve in response to societal exigencies, shifting power dynamics, and ideological transformations, thereby sculpting the political landscape and influencing public policies (Pipes, 1995).

Section 5: Social Structures and Societal Transformation

5.1 The Interplay of Social Change and Structures:

Social structures are not perpetual; they are dynamic entities subject to transformation over time (Eagleton, 2011). Social change can originate from various factors, including technological advancements, demographic transformations, cultural shifts, and social movements. These catalysts for change can reshape the organization, functioning, and even the disassembly of existing social structures and institutions (Tilly, 2004). During periods of rapid societal change, conflicts often arise as established norms clash with burgeoning ideologies and behavioral patterns.

5.2 Social Structures and Inequality:

Social structures are implicated in both perpetuating and mitigating social inequalities within a given society (Mills, 1956). Power dynamics and privilege structures frequently penetrate social systems, entrenching existing hierarchies and marginalizing specific social groups. For instance, racial, gender, and socioeconomic disparities may emerge from social structures that systematically privilege certain groups over others (Collins, 2000). Nonetheless, social structures can also evolve into arenas of resistance and transformation as individuals and movements mobilize to confront oppressive frameworks, advocating for social justice, equity, and inclusivity (Delgado & Stefancic, 2001). Structural changes and policy reforms can address existing inequalities, striving towards more equitable social institutions.

Conclusion:

This extensive chapter has afforded a comprehensive inquiry into social structures and institutions, illuminating their complex dynamics and profound repercussions for human behavior and societal organization. By comprehending the intricacies of social structures and institutions, we cultivate a richer understanding of societal organization, evolution, and transformation. Recognizing the interplay between individual agency and these overarching structures enables us to navigate the convolutions of our social worlds, fortifying our commitment to fostering more just, inclusive, and equitable societies.

***

Summary

We comprehensively explored social structures and institutions, examining their definitions, types (formal and informal), functions (regulation, socialization, resource distribution), examples (family, education, economy, politics), and their dynamic interplay with societal transformation and inequality.

Key Takeaways

- Social structures are intricate patterns of relationships and interactions within society, while institutions are established norms and practices shaping behavior.

- Social structures comprise roles, statuses, groups, and networks, influencing individual identities and actions.

- Formal structures are explicit systems (e.g., government), while informal structures emerge organically (e.g., friendship networks).

- Institutions fulfill crucial functions: regulation, socialization, and resource distribution.

- Examples of institutions include family, education, economic systems, and political systems.

- Social structures are dynamic and influence both the perpetuation and mitigation of social inequalities.

- Understanding social structures and institutions is key to comprehending societal organization, change, and pursuing more equitable societies.

***

QUESTIONS FOR FURTHER THOUGHT

1. Define social structures and institutions, and explain the key difference between them.

2. Identify and explain three constituents of social structures, providing examples for each.

3. Distinguish between formal and informal social structures, giving two examples of each and explaining their impact on society.

4. What are the three primary functions of social institutions? Explain each function with an example.

5. Discuss the role of the family as a social institution, highlighting its functions and variations across cultures.

6. Explain the role of education as a social institution, focusing on its contributions to socialization, social mobility, and its relationship to broader societal values.

7. How do economic institutions shape economic relationships, employment, and wealth distribution within a society? Provide examples of different types of economic systems.

8. Analyze the functions of political institutions, their role in social order, and their adaptability to societal changes.

9. Explain how social structures can both perpetuate and mitigate social inequalities, giving specific examples.

10. Describe the dynamic relationship between social structures, social change, and the potential for conflict during periods of rapid transformation.

References For Further Reading

1. Bott, E. (1971). *Family and Social Network.* Tavistock Publications.

2. Bowles, S., & Gintis, H. (1976). *Schooling in Capitalist America.* Basic Books.

3. Bourdieu, P. (1986). *The Forms of Capital.* In J. Richardson (Ed.), *Handbook of Theory and Research for the Sociology of Education* (pp. 241-258). Greenwood.

4. Collins, P. H. (2000). *Black Feminist Thought.* Routledge.

5. Coleman, J. S. (1990). *Foundations of Social Theory.* Harvard University Press.

6. Delgado, R., & Stefancic, J. (2001). *Critical Race Theory: An Introduction.* New York University Press.

7. Durkheim, E. (1984). *The Division of Labor in Society.* The Free Press. Eagleton, T. (2011). *Why Marx Was Right.* Yale University Press.

8. Eisenstadt, S. N. (1964). *Social Change.* Wiley.

9. Furstenberg, F. (2000). *The Unplanned Revolution: Changing Families in a Changing World.* In D. P. Moynihan (Ed.), *Social Democracy and the Family* (pp. 50-66). W. W. Norton.

10. Geertz, C. (1973). *The Interpretation of Cultures.* Basic Books.

11. Giddens, A. (1984). *The Constitution of Society*. University of California Press.

12. Giddens, A. (1993). *Sociology*. Polity Press.

13. Giddens, A. (2000). *Runaway World*. Routledge.

14. Granovetter, M. (1973). *The Strength of Weak Ties*. American Journal of Sociology, 78(6), 1360-1380.

15. Lasswell, H. D. (1950). *Politics: Who Gets What, When, How*. Whittlesey House.

16. Lucas, S. R. (2001). *Effectively Maintained Inequality: Educational Inequality, Status, and Social Capital*. American Journal of Sociology, 106(2), 332-362.

17. Mair, P. (2006). *Ruling the Void: The Hollowing of Western Democracy*. Verso.

18. Mills, C. W. (1956). *The Power Elite*. Oxford University Press.

19. North, D. C. (1990). *Institutions, Institutional Change and Economic Performance*. Cambridge University Press.

20. Parsons, T. (1951). *The Social System*. The Free Press.

21. Piketty, T. (2014). *Capital in the Twenty-First Century*. Belknap Press.

22. Pipes, R. (1995). *Russia Under the Bolshevik Regime*. Knopf.

23. Scott, W. R. (1995). *Organizations: Rational, Natural, and Open Systems*. Prentice Hall.

24. Searle, J. R. (1995). *The Construction of Social Reality*. The Free Press.

25. Simmel, G. (1971). *On Individuality and Social Forms*. University of Chicago Press.

26. Slaughter, S., & Rhoades, G. (2004). *Academic Capitalism and the New Economy: Markets, State, and Higher Education*. Johns Hopkins University Press.

27. Stiglitz, J. E. (2012). *The Price of Inequality: How Today's Divided Society Endangers Our Future*. W.W. Norton & Company.

28. Tilly, C. (2004). *Social Movements, 1768–2004*. Paradigm Publishers.

29. Turner, J. H. (2010). *Theoretical Principles of Sociology: Volume 1: Introduction to Sociological Theory*. Springer.

30. Weber, M. (1978). *Economy and Society: An Outline of Interpretive Sociology*. University of California Press.

31. Wasserman, S., & Faust, K. (1994). *Social Network Analysis: Methods and Applications*. Cambridge University Press.

Chapter Seven

Social Stratification and Inequality

Exploring the Intricacies of Social Stratification and Inequality

In this discourse, we shall embark on an exploration of the intricately layered and nuanced subject of social stratification and inequality. Our focus will encompass the structural frameworks within societies that form hierarchical systems influenced by an array of elements such as affluence, influence, social standing, and the complex dimensions of intersectionality (Marmot, 2005). Furthermore, we will scrutinize the genesis of social inequalities and their manifestations in diverse guises, ultimately deciphering their ramifications on individuals' prospects, quality of life, and holistic welfare (Piketty, 2014).

Comprehending Social Stratification

Social stratification delineates the segmentation of society into disparate tiers or strata, each characterized by varying degrees of access to resources, opportunities, and privileges (Giddens, 2000). These hierarchical structures are frequently underpinned by critical determinants such as economic class, professional engagement, educational attainment, social standing, and additional intersecting elements, including race, gender, and ethnicity (Bourdieu, 1987). The ramifications of social stratification are profound, influencing the lifestyles, social engagements, and ultimate life trajectories of individuals (Wilkinson & Pickett, 2010).

Manifestations of Inequality

In examining social stratification, it is imperative to acknowledge and dissect the myriad forms of inequality that permeate societal constructs. Economic inequality stands as a salient aspect, illuminating the disparities in wealth and income distribution. It is shaped by variables such as the concentration of capital, accessibility to education and employment avenues, technological evolution, globalization, and prevailing social policies (Piketty, 2014; Stiglitz, 2012). This economic divide can precipitate a cascade of consequences, including restricted resource allocation, unemployment, impoverishment, and societal discord, particularly for those languishing at the nadir of the social hierarchy (Bourguignon, 2015).

Occupational inequality scrutinizes the imbalanced distribution of employment opportunities alongside the contrasting remuneration and benefits of different vocations. This form of inequality often intersects with other dimensions—gender, race, ethnicity, and disability—resulting in a compounded effect (Reskin, 2012). Discrimination, entrenched biases, prevalent stereotypes, and disparities in hiring and promotion practices exacerbate the phenomenon of occupational stratification, constraining opportunities for individuals in marginalized factions and entrenching existing power structures (Bertrand & Mullainathan, 2004).

The inequality of social status investigates how individuals are appraised and valued based on their social backgrounds, educational attainments, accomplishments, and reservoirs of cultural capital (Bourdieu, 1984). Determinants of social status frequently include familial heritage, educational credentials, professional roles, and the social milieu one inhabits. Individuals occupying higher echelons of social status routinely enjoy a plethora of privileges, prestige, and social support, whereas those situated on the lower rungs often contend with prejudice, discrimination, and curtailed access to resources, opportunities, and networks (Thompson, 2012).

The Dynamics of Social Mobility

Social mobility encapsulates the flux of individuals or collectives from one social tier to another within the stratified system. It can manifest as upward mobility, involving ascension to superior social standings, or downward mobility, signifying a decline in position (Hout, 1988). Historically, certain societies have been characterized by substantial opportunities for social mobility, enabling individuals to ameliorate their circumstances. Nonetheless, the accessibility of social mobility is not universally equitable across all contexts, as various impediments frequently inhibit individual progress, thereby perpetuating systemic inequalities (Putnam, 2015).

Multiple classifications of social mobility exist. Structural mobility arises from overarching societal transformations, such as technological leaps or economic shifts, resulting in alterations within the general pattern of social stratification (Tilly, 1998). Intergenerational mobility pertains to the shifts in social positions that occur across familial generations, while intragenerational mobility denotes the transformations in an individual's social standing throughout their lifetime (Beller & Hout, 2006). These diverse modalities of mobility interrelate and collectively engender the overarching dynamics of social stratification within a society.

Theoretical Frameworks of Social Stratification

Sociologists have formulated various theories elucidating social stratification's origins and persistence. A notable perspective is Karl Marx's theory of class conflict, which accentuates the significance of economic factors and the contentious dynamics between the bourgeoisie (the capital-owning class) and the proletariat (the working class) (Marx & Engels, 1848). Marx contended that social stratification emerges from the unequal allocation of wealth and resources, sustained through exploitative relationships and maintained by the capitalist framework that inherently fosters social inequality.

Max Weber introduced a multidimensional approach to social stratification, emphasizing three critical dimensions: economic class, social status, and power (Weber, 1978). He posited that social stratification is shaped by both economic determinants and social hierarchies, which encompass prestige and social networks. According to Weber, power is a pivotal element in preserving and reproducing social inequality, shaping individuals' life chances regarding educational, employment, and socio-economic mobility opportunities.

Contemporary sociological theories have built upon these foundational constructs, integrating novel perspectives. Symbolic interactionism delves into how social meanings, interpretations, and interactions sculpt social stratification and inequality (Blumer, 1969). It underscores the pivotal role of symbols, language, and interpersonal exchanges in engendering and solidifying hierarchical constructs. Intersectionality theory sheds light on the confluence of various systems of oppression—based on gender, race, class, sexual orientation, and ability—which intertwine to influence individuals' social standings and their experiences of inequality (Crenshaw, 1989). This framework amplifies the significance of considering intersecting identities when analyzing social stratification and its attendant inequities.

Implications and Consequences

The implications of social stratification and inequality are profound, influencing both individual lives and societal structures at large. Disparate access to resources and opportunities fosters social exclusion, marginalization, and constrained life prospects for those ensconced in lower social tiers (Wilkinson & Pickett, 2009). The chasms in health outcomes, educational access, and discriminatory practices illustrate the deleterious consequences of entrenched social stratification.

The unequal availability of quality healthcare, nourishing sustenance, and secure living environments engenders significant health disparities among diverse social groups. Individuals burdened by lower social standing frequently encounter heightened incidences of chronic ailments diminished life expectancy, and suboptimal health outcomes (Marmot et al., 2008). Educational inequities further entrench social stratification by restricting individuals' access to superior educational opportunities, which are vital for upward mobility. Insufficient educational access can perpetuate existing hierarchies and stifle socio-economic advancement (Cascio & Schanzenbach, 2013).

Moreover, social inequality can incite social unrest, as marginalized populations may be galvanized to demand social and economic equity (Della Porta & Diani, 2006). Social movements—encompassing civil rights, feminist initiatives, LGBTQ+ advocacy, disability rights campaigns, and labor movements—have historically sought to challenge and dismantle entrenched societal inequalities (Tilly, 2004). These movements strive to cultivate more equitable frameworks wherein individuals possess equal opportunities for social, economic, and political engagement.

Conclusion

Social stratification and inequality represent ubiquitous phenomena within human societies. Understanding their origins, manifestations, and ramifications is essential for sociologists, policymakers, and the broader community. Through a meticulous analysis of the mechanisms that perpetuate inequality, societies can endeavor to construct more equitable structures and systems that afford all individuals equal possibilities for achievement, well-being, and social justice. Recognizing and proactively addressing the complexities of social stratification and inequality are indispensable steps toward fostering a fairer, more inclusive society for all.

***

Summary

We explored social stratification and inequality, examining its various forms (economic, occupational, social status), dynamics (social mobility), theoretical frameworks (Marx, Weber, symbolic interactionism, intersectionality), and consequences (health disparities, educational inequities, social unrest).

Key Takeaways

- Social stratification involves the hierarchical division of society into strata with varying access to resources and opportunities.

- Forms of inequality include economic disparity, unequal occupational distribution, and disparities in social status.

- Social upward and downward mobility is influenced by structural changes and individual efforts but is not always equally accessible.

- Theoretical perspectives on social stratification include Marx's class conflict, Weber's multidimensional approach, symbolic interactionism, and intersectionality theory.

- Social stratification has significant consequences, including health disparities, educational inequities, and the potential for social unrest.

- Addressing social stratification requires understanding its mechanisms and working toward creating more equitable societal structures.

***

QUESTIONS FOR FURTHER THOUGHT

1. Define social stratification and explain its key components.

2. Describe three forms of social inequality discussed in the text, providing examples of each.

3. Explain the concept of social mobility and distinguish between upward, downward, intergenerational, and intragenerational mobility.

4. Summarize Karl Marx's and Max Weber's theories of social stratification, highlighting their key differences.

5. Discuss the contributions of symbolic interactionism and intersectionality theory to understanding social stratification.

6. What are some of the implications and consequences of social stratification for individuals and society as a whole?

7. Explain how economic inequality contributes to other forms of inequality, such as occupational and social status inequality.

8. How do Educational inequities entrench social stratification?

9. Describe the relationship between social structures, social change, and potential conflict.

10. Based on the text, what are some potential strategies for reducing social stratification and promoting greater equality?

***

References For Further Reading

1. Beller, E., & Hout, M. (2006). Intergenerational social mobility: The United States in comparative perspective. *Future of Children*, 16(2), 19-36.

2. Bertrand, M., & Mullainathan, S. (2004). Are Emily and

Greg More Employable than Lakisha and Jamal? A Field Experiment on Labor Market Discrimination. *American Economic Review*, 94(4), 991-1013.

3. Blumer, H. (1969). *Symbolic Interactionism: Perspective and Method.* University of California Press.

4. Bourdieu, P. (1984). *Distinction: A Social Critique of the Judgement of Taste.* Harvard University Press.

5. Bourdieu, P. (1987). *Categories and the Economy.* In P. Bourdieu & J. Coleman (Eds.), *Social Theory for a Changing Society* (pp. 23-40). Westview Press.

6. Bourguignon, F. (2015). *The Globalization of the Inequality: Theoretical and Methodological Issues.* In *Measuring Global Inequality* (pp. 5-34). Palgrave Macmillan.

7. Cascio, E. U., & Schanzenbach, D. W. (2013). The Effect of School Quality on Students' Long-Term Earnings: Evidence from a Randomized Experiment. *Review of Economics and Statistics*, 95(3), 911-927.

8. Crenshaw, K. (1989). Demarginalizing the Intersection of Race and Sex: A Black Feminist Critique of Antidiscrimination Doctrine, Feminist Theory and Antiracist Politics. *University of Chicago Legal Forum*, 1989(1), 139-167.

9. Della Porta, D., & Diani, M. (2006). *Social Movements: An Introduction.* Blackwell Publishing.

10. Giddens, A. (2000). *Sociology.* Polity Press.

11. Hout, M. (1988). More Divided Than Ever? Changes in Earnings Distribution in the U.S., 1967–1986. *Sociological Forum*, 3(4), 679-694.

12. Marmot, M. (2005). Social determinants of health inequalities. *The Lancet*, 365(9464), 1099-1104.

13. Marmot, M., Stansfeld, S., Patel, C., and Fat, L.S. (2008). Health inequalities among British civil servants: the Whitehall II study. *The Lancet*, 372(9650), 1655-1663.

14. Marx, K., & Engels, F. (1848). *The Communist Manifesto.*

15. Piketty, T. (2014). *Capital in the Twenty-First Century.* Belknap Press.

16. Putnam, R. D. (2015). *Our Kids: The American Dream in Crisis.* Simon & Schuster.

17. Reskin, B. F. (2012). The Race Discrimination System. *American Sociological Review*, 77(4), 695-718.

18. Scott, J. (1995). *Social Network Analysis: A Handbook.* Sage Publications.

19. Stiglitz, J. E. (2012). *The Price of Inequality: How Today's Divided Society Endangers Our Future.* W.W. Norton & Company.

20. Thompson, M. (2012). Social Status and Health: Evidence from the National Longitudinal Health Survey. *Sociology of Health & Illness*, 34(8), 1241-1260.

21. Tilly, C. (1998). *Durable Inequality.* University of California Press.

22. Tilly, C. (2004). *Social Movements, 1768–2004.* Paradigm Publishers.

23. Weber, M. (1978). *Economy and Society: An Outline of Interpretive Sociology.* University of California Press.

24. Wilkinson, R., & Pickett, K. (2009). *The Spirit Level: Why Equality is Better for Everyone.* Penguin.

25. Wilkinson, R., & Pickett, K. (2010). *The Spirit Level: Why More Equal Societies Almost Always Do Better.* Allen Lane.

Chapter Eight

Culture and Society

The Interwoven Dynamics of Culture and Society

In this chapter, we will delve into the intricate relationship between culture and society. Culture encapsulates the shared customs, beliefs, values, and behaviors that define a particular group or society, while society represents the broader social framework within which individuals and groups interact (Giddens, 2000). A nuanced exploration of the dynamic interplay between culture and society is essential for understanding social processes and how individuals shape and are shaped by their environments (Durkheim, 1984).

Defining Culture

Culture is a multifaceted construct comprising many elements, including language, art, music, literature, cuisine, rituals, traditions, religious beliefs, and social norms (Hofstede, 2001). These components inform how individuals perceive, interpret, and engage with the world around them. Culture is not a static entity but a dynamic and adaptive system that evolves in response to various internal and external influences (Kroeber & Kluckhohn, 1952).

At its essence, culture furnishes a framework for understanding and navigating the complexities of existence. It empowers individuals to make sense of their surroundings, establish social norms, and engage in meaningful communication (Geertz, 1973). Language, a vital aspect of culture, facilitates the transmission of knowledge and ideas across generations, enabling societies to accumulate and build upon the collective wisdom of their ancestors (Whorf, 1956).

The Reciprocity of Culture and Society

Culture and society exist in a state of continuous interaction, profoundly influencing and reshaping each other (Berger & Luckmann, 1967). Society is the backdrop against which culture develops, while culture simultaneously informs societal structures and institutions. This relationship is not unidirectional; rather, it embodies a dynamic and reciprocal process that unfolds through individuals' intricate experiences (Eagleton, 2011).

Social norms, values, and institutions shape cultural practices, while cultural beliefs and customs are the foundation for societal constructs. For instance, religious beliefs often inform the moral codes and ethical principles that underpin societal expectations (Durkheim, 1915). Similarly, cultural values mold political, economic, and educational frameworks, reflecting the deep interconnection between cultural content and social organization (Weber, 1978).

Cultural Universals: Common Threads Amidst Diversity

Despite the significant variations between cultures, certain universal elements are present in nearly every society. These fundamental aspects, known as cultural universals, include language, family structures, marriage customs, educational systems, and religious beliefs (Murdock, 1945). While these universals' specific forms and expressions vary widely, their presence in all societies underscores the shared patterns that characterize human social existence.

Language exemplifies a cultural universal that facilitates communication and social interaction (Sapir, 1921). Although the languages spoken around the globe differ markedly, they share underlying structures and fulfill the common human need for expression and connection. Likewise, family systems, despite their diverse structures and dynamics, serve as the primary unit for socialization, support, and reproduction across all societies (Bengtson, 2001).

The Lens of Cultural Relativism

Cultural relativism is a pivotal philosophical concept in studying culture and society. It posits that cultural practices, values, and beliefs should be understood and assessed within the specific context of their cultural origins (Boas, 1940). This perspective encourages individuals to suspend judgment and appreciate the rich diversity of cultural expressions, recognizing that no culture holds an inherent superiority or inferiority over another (Cultural relativism, 2019).

By adopting a culturally relative viewpoint, we can more profoundly grasp the complexities of human existence and the intricate tapestry of cultural diversity. Cultures provide unique frameworks through which individuals interpret their experiences and construct meaning. Embracing cultural relativism fosters a more nuanced understanding of diverse practices and facilitates meaningful intercultural dialogue and exchange (Cushner & Koch, 2002).

The Mechanisms of Cultural Change and Diffusion

Cultural change arises as societies encounter novel ideas, technologies, and interactions with other societies. Cultural diffusion—whereby cultural elements spread from one society to another—plays a vital role in this transformation (Spread of Culture, 2015). Such diffusion can occur through trade, migration, media, and technological advancements, leading to adopting, adapting, or rejecting new cultural practices (Hannerz, 1990).

The concept of cultural evolution acknowledges that cultures are not fixed entities but develop and transform over time (Nisbet, 1969). As societies experience social, economic, and technological shifts, their cultural practices and beliefs adapt to accommodate new realities. However, it is essential to recognize that cultural change does not necessarily signify progress or improvement; it can yield both beneficial and detrimental outcomes for individuals and societies (Inglehart & Welzel, 2005).

Culture, Identity, and Socialization

Culture is integral in shaping both individual and collective identities. It provides a lens through which we understand ourselves and others, as our values, beliefs, and behaviors are cultivated and internalized through socialization processes within cultural contexts (Mead, 1934). Socialization serves as the mechanism through which individuals acquire the skills, knowledge, and norms necessary for participation in society. Through socialization, culture becomes interwoven into our identities, influencing our thoughts, actions, and relationships (Bourdieu, 1984).

Socialization begins at birth and continues throughout life, occurring within various social institutions, including the family unit, educational systems, media, and peer groups (Bronfenbrenner, 1979). These institutions are crucial in transmitting cultural values, norms, and practices that shape our sense of self and our interactions with others. While individual identities are influenced by culture, they are also shaped by personal experiences and choices, signifying a complex interplay between them.

Navigating Cultural Diversity and Conflict

Cultural diversity is a fundamental characteristic of human societies. When different cultures intersect, conflicts may arise due to divergent beliefs, values, and practices (Moghadam, 2005). Consequently, balancing cultural diversity while promoting tolerance to foster social cohesion and peaceful coexistence is imperative. Societies must address these conflicts through constructive dialogue, understanding, and respect for cultural differences (Huntington, 1993).

Globalization has intensified cultural interactions, facilitating increased interconnectedness and mobility. While this fosters opportunities for cross-cultural learning and appreciation, it also poses challenges, as clashes of values and interests may emerge (Appadurai, 1996). Bridging these cultural divides necessitates intentional efforts to promote intercultural understanding, empathy, and open-mindedness. By nurturing intercultural awareness and respect, societies can foster unity and enhance their social fabric (Sullivan, 2009).

Conclusion

The interplay between culture and society is profound, with each shaping and influencing the other in manifold ways. By expanding our comprehension of culture's role within society, we gain deeper insight into the richness of human experience and the diversity of social systems. Recognizing cultural patterns and values facilitates a better understanding of the intricacies involved in social interactions, paving the way toward a more inclusive and harmonious world. Embracing cultural diversity and fostering cross-cultural understanding empowers us to construct bridges rather than barriers, thus nurturing a society that celebrates the beauty inherent in our shared humanity.

***

Summary

We explored the intricate relationship between culture and society, defining culture's multifaceted elements, examining their reciprocal influence, and discussing cultural universals, relativism, change, and its role in shaping identity.

Key Takeaways

- Culture encompasses shared beliefs, values, and behaviors defining a group or society, while society provides the interaction framework.
- Culture and society interact dynamically, with each shap-

ing the other and influencing social structures and institutions.

- Cultural universals, like language and family structures, exist across societies despite variations in their forms.

- Cultural relativism promotes understanding diverse cultural practices without judgment.

- Cultural change and diffusion occur through various means, leading to adaptation and evolution.

- Culture significantly shapes individual and collective identities through socialization.

- Navigating cultural diversity and potential conflicts requires promoting tolerance and intercultural understanding.

***

QUESTIONS FOR FURTHER THOUGHT

1. Define culture and society, explaining their key differences and providing examples.

2. Explain the concept of cultural relativism and its importance in understanding diverse societies.

3. Identify and explain three cultural universals, giving examples of how they manifest differently across cultures.

4. Describe the dynamic relationship between culture and society, illustrating how they mutually influence each

other.

5. Discuss the role of socialization in shaping individual identities within a cultural context.

6. Explain how cultural diffusion contributes to cultural change, providing examples of mechanisms through which it occurs.

7. Analyze the potential for conflict arising from cultural diversity, and suggest strategies for promoting intercultural understanding and tolerance.

8. What are the key components of culture? Provide examples to illustrate your answer.

9. Discuss the concept of cultural universals and their significance in understanding shared human experiences, despite cultural variations.

10. Explain how social institutions contribute to transmitting cultural values and norms and how this impacts socialization.

References For Further Reading

1. Appadurai, A. (1996). *Modernity at Large: Cultural Dimensions of Globalization.* University of Minnesota Press.

2. Bengtson, V. L. (2001). *Beyond the Nuclear Family: The Increasing Importance of Extended Family in American Society.* In V. L. Bengtson, P. N. Antonucci, & J. B. B. Silverstein (Eds.), *Handbook of Theories of Aging.* Springer.

3. Berger, P. L., & Luckmann, T. (1967). *The Social Construction of Reality: A Treatise in the Sociology of Knowledge.* Anchor Books.

4. Bourdieu, P. (1984). *Distinction: A Social Critique of the Judgement of Taste.* Harvard University Press.

5. Boas, F. (1940). *Race, Language, and Culture.* University of Chicago Press.

6. Bronfenbrenner, U. (1979). *The Ecology of Human Development: Experiments by Nature and Design.* Harvard University Press.

7. Cushner, K. H., & Koch, P. T. (2002). *Why Culture Matters: A Guide to Cross-Cultural Communication in the Classroom.* International Society for Technology in Education.

8. Duncan, O. D., & Puma, J. C. (2016). *The Measurement of Social Inequality.* In R. K. Merton (Ed.), *On Social Inequality: A Historical Perspective.* Transaction Publishers.

9. Durkheim, E. (1984). *The Division of Labor in Society.*

The Free Press.

10. Eagleton, T. (2011). *Why Marx Was Right.* Yale University Press.

11. Geertz, C. (1973). *The Interpretation of Cultures.* Basic Books.

12. Giddens, A. (2000). *Sociology.* Polity Press.

13. Hannerz, U. (1990). *Flows and Contradictions in a Global Setting.* In M. Featherstone (Ed.), *Global Culture: Nationalism, Globalization and Modernity* (pp. 38-56). Sage Publications.

14. Hofstede, G. (2001). *Culture's Consequences: Comparing Values, Behaviors, Institutions, and Organizations Across Nations.* Sage Publications.

15. Huntington, S. P. (1993). *The Clash of Civilizations?* Foreign Affairs, 72(3), 22-49.

16. Inglehart, R., & Welzel, C. (2005). *Modernization, Cultural Change, and Democracy: The Human Development Sequence.* Cambridge University Press.

17. Kroeber, A. L., & Kluckhohn, C. (1952). *Culture: A Critical Review of Concepts and Definitions.* American Anthropologist, 55(4), 1-42.

18. Mead, G. H. (1934). *Mind, Self, and Society from the Standpoint of a Social Behaviorist.* University of Chicago Press.

19. Moghadam, V. M. (2005). *From 'Women and Development' to 'Gender and Development': Theoretical Perspec-*

tives on Gender and Development. In *Gender and Development in the Global Economy* (pp. 11-24). Zed Books.

20. Murdock, G. P. (1945). *The Common Denominator of Cultures.* American Anthropologist, 47(1), 43-57.

21. Nisbet, R. A. (1969). *The Sociological Tradition.* Basic Books.

22. Sapir, E. (1921). *Language: An Introduction to the Study of Speech.* Harcourt, Brace & Co.

23. Spread of Culture (2015). *Cultural Diffusion in Anthropology.* Encyclopedia of Anthropology.

24. Sullivan, M. (2009). *The Role of Culture in Peacebuilding: Culture, Religion, and Conflict Resolution.* International Journal of Peace Studies, 14(1), 23-38.

25. Whorf, B. L. (1956). *Language, Thought, and Reality: Selected Writings of Benjamin Lee Whorf.* MIT Press.

26. Weber, M. (1978). *Economy and Society: An Outline of Interpretive Sociology.* University of California Press.

Chapter Nine

Sociology of Religion

Exploring the Sociology of Religion: Theories, Concepts, and Case Studies

THE STUDY OF RELIGION occupies a pivotal position in the field of sociology. By scrutinizing the social dimensions of religious beliefs, practices, and institutions, sociologists endeavor to elucidate religion's significant role in shaping both individuals and the fabric of society (Modood, 2016). The sociology of religion provides illuminating insights into the interplay between religion and social interactions, cultural norms, and even political frameworks (Swatos & Christiano, 1999). In this chapter, we will examine the primary theoretical paradigms, research methodologies, key concepts, and notable case studies that define the sociology of religion.

Theoretical Perspectives

Sociologists adopt a range of theoretical perspectives to comprehensively analyze the functions of religion within the societal context (Bryant, 2010). Let us explore these perspectives in detail.

a) **Functionalism**

The functionalist perspective focuses on the role of religion in reinforcing social order and cohesion. It emphasizes religion's ability to give individuals a shared set of values and beliefs (Durkheim, 1995). Émile Durkheim proposed that religion acts as a collective representation of society's moral convictions and norms, fostering a sense of solidarity among its adherents (Durkheim, 1912). Religious rituals and ceremonies cultivate social bonds and engender a sense of belonging, thereby supporting a collective consciousness that aids individuals in navigating the complexities of social existence. Similarly, Robert K. Merton posited that religion is crucial in providing meaning and purpose in life by addressing existential queries and nurturing a sense of identity (Merton, 1968).

b) **Conflict Theory**

The conflict perspective interrogates the power dynamics inherent in religious institutions and how they may perpetuate social hierarchies and inequalities. Karl Marx famously described religion as the "opium of the masses," suggesting that it serves to pacify the oppressed, distracting them from their exploitation (Marx, 1844). From this vantage point, religion can obscure social inequalities and perpetuate prevailing ideologies. Feminist theorists, drawing from conflict theory, have scrutinized the ways in which religious discourses and practices reinforce gender inequalities by perpetuating traditional gender roles and limiting women's agency (Tong, 2009). They analyze how patriarchal structures are often woven into religious institutions, thereby affecting women's social standings and opportunities.

c) **Symbolic Interactionism**

The symbolic interactionist perspective centers on the individual experiences and meanings associated with religious beliefs and practices (Blumer, 1969). Erving Goffman's dramaturgical approach posits that individuals engage in impression management during religious rituals, presenting themselves favorably to others and conforming to social norms and expectations (Goffman, 1959). This perspective emphasizes how symbols and rituals shape religious identity and community. Symbolic interactionists examine how individuals negotiate and construct their religious identities through social interactions and engagement in religious rituals, illuminating the role that religious symbols, rituals, and language play in forging interpersonal relationships and establishing shared understandings within religious communities (Hervieu-Léger, 2000).

Research Methods

Sociologists employ a variety of research methodologies to investigate the sociology of religion. Let's examine these methods in further detail.

a) **Surveys and Interviews**

Surveys and interviews facilitate the collection of data regarding individuals' religious beliefs, practices, and affiliations, shedding light on the diversity and prevalence of religious experiences (Casanova, 1994). These methods explore correlations with factors such as social class, education, and ethnicity, which may influence religious beliefs and practices. Surveys yield quantitative data, while interviews offer qualitative insights, allowing researchers to delve into individuals' subjective experiences and perspectives on their religious lives (Smith, 2009).

b) **Ethnography**

Ethnographic research proves invaluable in the sociology of religion, as it enables sociologists to immerse themselves in religious communities, observing rituals, interactions, and symbols firsthand (Hannerz, 1993). This immersive approach fosters a deeper understanding of the social significance of religious practices. Through prolonged engagement and participant observation, ethnographers capture the nuances and complexities of religious life, examining how religion shapes social interactions and forges connections within specific cultural contexts (Wuthnow, 2005).

c) **Historical Analysis**

Historical analysis is utilized to investigate the development and transformations of religious institutions across time (Casanova, 1994). By tracing the historical trajectories of religious beliefs and practices, sociologists can discern patterns, understand shifts in religious influence, and evaluate how socio-economic and political changes interface with religious phenomena (van der Meer, 2009). This method provides crucial context for analyzing the social, cultural, and political environments in which religions emerge, evolve, and interact with other social institutions.

Key Concepts

Several key concepts are foundational to the sociology of religion. Let us explore these concepts in greater detail.

a) **Religious Socialization**

Religious socialization refers to how individuals absorb religious beliefs, values, and behaviors through interactions with religious institutions, family, and peers (Burgess, 1988). This process is integral to the formation of religious identities and significantly influences individuals' worldviews. Religious socialization aids in transmitting cultural traditions and integrates individuals into broader societal norms and values (Houtman & Aupers, 2007). Through this process, individuals learn about their religious communities' rituals, symbols, and doctrines, fostering a sense of belonging and commitment.

b) Religious Pluralism

Religious pluralism examines the coexistence of diverse religions within societies and explores the social dynamics that arise from such diversity (Tschannen, 1999). It analyzes interactions, competition, and negotiation among religious communities. While religious pluralism can cultivate tolerance, interfaith dialogue, and new social movements, it may also incite conflicts and power struggles between various religious groups, challenging the dominance of certain traditions (Wuthnow, 1988). Sociologists focused on religious pluralism investigate the social and political dynamics shaping interactions and power relations among different faith communities.

c) Secularization

Secularization denotes the declining influence of organized religion within society, characterized by a waning emphasis on religious beliefs and practices in individuals' lives (Wilson, 1982). Émile Durkheim theorized that as societies grow more complex and specialized, religious influences yield to other collective representations, such as science and the state (Durkheim, 1912). In contrast, Max Weber argued that the rationalization process inherent in modernity has disenfranchised religious outlooks, weakening the grip of religious institutions (Weber, 1978). Sociologists exploring secularization analyze how societal transformations—such as urbanization, industrialization, and advancements in scientific rationality—impact individuals' religious beliefs and practices, alongside the broader social implications of diminishing religious authority (Dobbelaere, 2002).

Case Studies

Throughout history, a variety of case studies illuminate the sociology of religion. Let's examine several significant case studies in depth.

a) The Protestant Reformation

The Protestant Reformation, initiated by Martin Luther in the 16th century, represented a watershed moment in religious history, challenging the authority and doctrines of the Catholic Church and resulting in the emergence of numerous Protestant denominations (MacCulloch, 2003). This movement not only spurred theological shifts but also instigated transformative social changes, including the decentralization of religious authority, heightened literacy and education among Protestants, and the rise of novel social and political dynamics. Sociologists investigating the Protestant Reformation analyze the intersections between religious beliefs and practices and broader social, political, and economic transformations within European societies and beyond (Stark, 2003).

b) Rise of New Religious Movements

The emergence of new religious movements in the 19th and 20th centuries—such as the Mormons, Jehovah's Witnesses, and various charismatic groups—illustrates the adaptability of religious beliefs in response to social and cultural shifts (Campbell & Tsurumi, 2004). These movements often arise as reactions to perceived social inequalities, political turmoil, or the quest for alternative spiritual paths among disaffected individuals. Sociological studies of new religious movements examine the social factors fostering their emergence, the distinct beliefs and practices they espouse, and their interactions with established religious institutions and mainstream societal values (Bromley & Melton, 2002).

c) **Religious Fundamentalism**

Religious fundamentalism is characterized by a conservative, literal interpretation of religious texts and doctrines, often emerging in reaction to perceived threats posed by secularism, modernity, or globalization (Martin, 2005). Sociologists analyzing religious fundamentalism explore its social and political ramifications, including impacts on gender roles, social policies, and intergroup relations (Marty & Appleby, 1991). They investigate processes of radicalization and the motivations propelling violent acts purportedly motivated by religious beliefs (Hoffman, 2006).

Conclusion

The sociology of religion provides profound insights into how religion influences and is influenced by social structures, cultural values, and individual experiences (Hervieu-Léger, 2000). Through diverse theoretical paradigms, research methodologies, and an exploration of foundational concepts and significant case studies, sociologists deepen their understanding of religion's role in shaping society. The study of the sociology of religion offers a robust framework for examining the dynamics of religious beliefs and practices, religious institutions, and the broader social, cultural, and political contexts surrounding them (Casanova, 2006). By engaging with these complexities, sociologists contribute to a richer comprehension of religion's vital role in human affairs.

***

Summary

We explored the sociology of religion, examining theoretical perspectives (functionalism, conflict theory, symbolic interactionism), research methods (surveys, ethnography, historical analysis), key concepts (religious socialization, pluralism, secularization), and case studies (the Protestant Reformation, new religious movements, religious fundamentalism) to understand religion's role in shaping society.

Key Takeaways

- The sociology of religion examines religion's influence on individuals and society.

- Three major theoretical perspectives—functionalism, conflict theory, and symbolic interactionism—offer different lenses for analyzing religion.

- Sociologists utilize surveys, interviews, ethnography, and historical analysis to study religion.

- Key concepts include religious socialization, religious pluralism, and secularization.

- Case studies such as the Protestant Reformation and the rise of new religious movements illustrate the dynamic interplay between religion and society.

- We concluded by highlighting the multifaceted role of religion in shaping human affairs.

***

QUESTIONS FOR FURTHER THOUGHT

1. Explain the three main theoretical perspectives (function-

alism, conflict theory, and symbolic interactionism) used in the sociology of religion, providing examples of each from the text.

2. Describe two sociological research methods used to study religion and explain their strengths and weaknesses.

3. Define "religious socialization" and explain its importance in shaping individual religious identities and societal values.

4. What is religious pluralism, and how can it lead to both positive and negative social outcomes?

5. Define "secularization" and discuss contrasting perspectives on its causes and consequences, referencing Durkheim's and Weber's contributions.

6. Summarize the key arguments and significance of the Protestant Reformation as a case study in the sociology of religion.

7. Explain the sociological interest in the rise of new religious movements, highlighting factors contributing to their emergence.

8. What are the defining characteristics of religious fundamentalism, and what are some of its social and political implications, as discussed in the text?

9. Identify and explain three key concepts fundamental to the sociology of religion, using examples to illustrate their application.

10. Based on the provided text, how does the sociology of religion contribute to a deeper understanding of the re-

lationship between religion and society?

References For Further Reading

1. Blumer, H. (1969). Symbolic Interactionism: Perspective and Method.

2. Bromley, D. G., & Melton, J. G. (2002). Cults, Religion, and Violence.

3. Bryant, C. G. A. (2010). The Sociology of Religion.

4. Burgess, R. G. (1988). Keeping Research: A Guide to the Sociology of Religion.

5. Campbell, C., & Tsurumi, K. (2004). The New Religious Movements Experience in America.

6. Casanova, J. (1994). Public Religions in the Modern World.

7. Casanova, J. (2006). The Secular, Secularizations, Secularism.

8. Dobbelaere, K. (2002). Secularization: A Multifaceted Resource.

9. Durkheim, É. (1912). The Elementary Forms of Religious Life.

10. Durkheim, É. (1995). The Division of Labor in Society.

11. Goffman, E. (1959). The Presentation of Self in Everyday Life.

12. Hannerz, U. (1993). Cultural Complexity: Studies in the

Social Organization of Meaning.

13. Hervieu-Léger, D. (2000). Religion as a Chain of Memory.

14. Hoffman, B. (2006). Inside Terrorism.

15. Houtman, D., & Aupers, S. (2007). The Spiritual Turn and the Decline of Tradition: The Spread of Postmodern Spirituality in Contemporary Western Society.

16. MacCulloch, D. (2003). The Reformation: A History.

17. Marty, M. E., & Appleby, R. S. (1991). Fundamentalisms Observed.

18. Marx, K. (1844). The Critique of Hegel's Philosophy of Right.

19. Merton, R. K. (1968). Social Theory and Social Structure.

20. Martin, S. (2005). The Future of Religion: Secularization, Revival, and the Merchandising of Religion.

21. Stark, R. (2003). For the Glory of God: How Monotheism Led to Reformation, Science, Witch-Hunts, and the End of Slavery.

22. Swatos, W. H., & Christiano, K. J. (1999). Secularization Theory: Measurement and Explanation.

23. Tong, R. (2009). Feminist Thought: A More Comprehensive Introduction.

24. Tschannen, O. (1999). The Politics of Secularization: Religion and Politics in Contemporary Society.

25. van der Meer, T. (2009). The Study of the Historical Foundations of Religion.

26. Weber, M. (1978). Economy and Society.

27. Wilson, B. (1982). Religion in Sociological Perspective.

28. Wuthnow, R. (1988). The American Synagogue: A Historical and Contemporary Perspective.

29. Wuthnow, R. (2005). Saving America: Faith-Based Services and the Future of Civil Society.

Chapter Ten

Deviance and Crime

The Exegesis of Deviance and Crime in Sociological Discourse

Deviance and crime are inextricably woven into the societal tapestry, captivating the scrutiny of sociologists across epochs. This discourse endeavors to unearth the intricacies of these concepts and elucidate their profound influence on social interactions and institutional dynamics (Merton, 1968). We shall traverse the multifaceted theories of deviance, examine the societal construction of crime, and scrutinize the ramifications of collective responses to deviant actions on individuals and communities. By concentrating on the socio-cultural milieu and the implications of deviance and crime, we aspire to illuminate their pivotal roles within the societal framework.

Elucidating Deviance

Deviance encapsulates behaviors or actions that diverge from the established societal norms and expectations. It is paramount to recognize that deviance is not an intrinsic attribute of an action; rather, it embodies a sociocultural appraisal affixed by society (Becker, 1963). Normative structures delineate acceptable conduct, and deviation manifests when individuals or collectives transgress these established boundaries. While some forms of deviance may be benign—such as the adoption of unconventional fashion choices or the embrace of alternative lifestyles—others wield substantial repercussions, manifesting in grave criminal transgressions or acts of violence (Sutherland, 1949).

Deviance can be bifurcated into formal and informal categories. Formal deviance pertains to violations of explicit legal statutes, culminating in judicial repercussions. Conversely, informal deviance involves breaches of social constructs without recourse to the legal apparatus (Cohen, 1955). Grasping these distinctions facilitates a nuanced analysis of societal reactions and the implications that ensue from deviant behaviors.

Theoretical Paradigms of Deviance

A plethora of theoretical frameworks endeavor to elucidate the antecedents and ramifications of deviant behavior. A salient paradigm is the functionalist perspective, positing that deviance serves critical functions within society (Durkheim, 1895). This perspective argues that deviance aids in delineating and reaffirming societal norms, thus bolstering the maintenance of social order. When individuals observe the repercussions of deviant conduct, they are often reminded of the necessity of conforming to societal expectations, functioning as a mechanism of social control.

In contradistinction, the conflict perspective emphasizes the interplay of power discrepancies and social inequities in the genesis of deviance (Marx & Engels, 1848). From this vantage point, the classifications of deviance and criminality are not impartially applied; rather, they are selectively influenced by social, economic, and political determinants. Those wielding power within the societal hierarchy cultivate definitions of deviant and criminal actions favoring their interests, often marginalizing or criminalizing disadvantaged groups (Alexander, 2010). For instance, in numerous jurisdictions, specific narcotic policies disproportionately target racial and ethnic minorities, thereby perpetuating systemic inequalities (Mauer, 2006).

Moreover, the symbolic interactionist perspective delves into the interpretative frameworks individuals utilize when ascribing meaning to deviant and criminal behaviors (Blumer, 1969). Proponents of symbolic interactionism contend that deviance is not inherently existent in an action; instead, it is socially constructed through interactions among individuals, groups, and the societal milieu. The labeling theory—central to this paradigm—postulates that individuals designated as deviant or criminal may internalize these labels, fostering a self-fulfilling prophecy that precipitates further deviant conduct (Lemert, 1951).

The Societal Construction of Crime

Similar to deviance, the concept of crime is an artifact of social constructs (Tannenbaum, 1938). What delineates an act as criminal varies across different societies and temporal contexts. The legal system is instrumental in adjudicating which actions are deemed criminal; legislators and enforcement bodies interpret and implement the law (Cohen, 1985). These legal classifications are influenced by cultural, historical, and political contexts, intricately reflecting the interests and values of those in dominion over defining and enforcing laws (Tonry, 1995). It is imperative to scrutinize critically the cultural and social context wherein crime is delineated, appreciating that crime is not an objective category but a byproduct of societal construction.

Public perceptions of crime are significantly influenced by media portrayal, often engendering moral panics and the criminalization of distinct demographics or behaviors (Cohen, 1972). Media depictions tend to sensationalize and emphasize violent acts, distorting public perception and influencing policy formulation. Stereotyping informed by race, ethnicity, and socio-economic status perpetuates entrenched biases, resulting in disparate treatment within the criminal justice apparatus (Reiner, 2007). An astute understanding of the media's role and public discourse is critical for analyzing the constructs surrounding crime and the ensuing consequences on marginalized communities.

Societal Responses to Deviance

The societal response to deviance encompasses a broad spectrum of mechanisms, oscillating from informal social sanctions to formal legal interventions (Goffman, 1963). Informal societal responses, such as gossip, ostracism, or public shaming, act as deterrents while reinforcing prevailing norms (Rock, 2007). These informal modes of social control are crucial for sustaining social order and cohesion, hinging upon communal pressure and individual accountability.

Conversely, formal control mechanisms such as the criminal justice system endeavor to uphold social order by penalizing and rehabilitating individuals who engage in deviant or criminal acts (Tonry, 1995). However, the criminal justice system is not insulated from the biases engrained within society. Disenfranchised groups frequently encounter disproportionate law enforcement scrutiny, biased arrest rates, and more severe punitive measures compared to their privileged counterparts. This phenomenon, termed systemic or institutionalized racism and discrimination, mirrors structural inequities perpetuated within the criminal justice framework—obscuring pathways for rehabilitation and reintegration (Alexander, 2010).

Recent years have witnessed the emergence of restorative justice paradigms gaining traction (Zehr, 2002). This approach prioritizes the remediation of harm inflicted by criminal activities and the subsequent reintegration of individuals into the community. It underscores dialogue, accountability, and mediation among victims, offenders, and their communities, striving to fulfill the restorative needs of all parties involved. Proponents ardently argue that restorative justice embodies a more transformative and healing approach in contrast to traditional punitive frameworks (Benson, 2013).

Deviance, Crime, and the Catalyst for Social Change

Deviance and crime operate as dynamic agents of social transformation. Deviant acts can challenge entrenched power structures and normative frameworks, inciting movements for social reform. Historical paradigms of rebellion, protest, and civil disobedience have indelibly contributed to social progress (Tilly, 2004). For example, the civil rights movement in the United States epitomized a challenge to racial segregation, catalyzing pivotal legal and social transformations (Morris, 1984). Similarly, the LGBTQ+ rights movement has valiantly fought against systemic discrimination and societal prejudice, engendering greater acceptance and acknowledgment of this community's rights (Armstrong, 2005).

Analyzing crime rates can yield valuable insights into sociopolitical conditions, often serving as a precursor for policy alterations (Tonry, 1995). High incidences of specific criminal activities, such as theft or drug-related offenses, frequently highlight underlying societal maladies such as poverty, inequality, and inadequate access to essential resources. A profound understanding of the root causes of crime enables informed policy decisions that address these structural disparities and work toward social and economic equity (Mauer, 2006).

Nevertheless, it is vital to understand the intricate relationship between deviance, crime, and social change; not all acts of deviance or criminality yield progressive outcomes. Social movements embody dual facets—capable of both beneficial reform and detrimental repercussions, contingent upon their objectives and methodologies (Armstrong & Crage, 2006). Furthermore, the categorization of an action as deviant or criminal should transcend mere societal consensus; it must consider the contextual intricacies and the potential for substantive social change.

Conclusion

Deviance and crime emerge as intricate phenomena demanding thorough sociological inquiry. By illuminating the social dimensions and implications of deviant conduct and crime, we deepen our comprehension of societal dynamics, alongside the methods by which norms and laws materialize and are upheld. This discourse endeavors to furnish a nuanced understanding of the complexities surrounding deviance and crime, encompassing a spectrum of theoretical perspectives on deviance while emphasizing how societal reactions and power modalities shape the labeling and treatment of individuals engaged in deviant or criminal behavior.

The intricate social construction of crime has been duly examined, accentuating how cultural, historical, and political contingencies construct the definitions and classifications of criminality. We have also scrutinized diverse societal responses to deviance, spanning informal sanctions to formal legal measures, recognizing the systemic inequities that pervade the criminal justice landscape and hinder rehabilitative pursuits.

Moreover, we acknowledge the potentiality of deviance and crime to serve as catalysts for social transformation. Deviance often acts as a formidable force in contesting prevailing norms and power dynamics, engendering significant social movements and reforms (Tilly, 2004). Additionally, a robust comprehension of the root causes of crime can inform policy initiatives that rectify underlying social inequities, striving for a more equitable and just society.

As we study deviance and crime, a critical lens is indispensable, seeking to reveal the contexts and social factors influencing their emergence. This inquiry cultivates a sophisticated understanding of the convoluted interplay between individuals, society, and the construction of behaviors deemed deviant or criminal. By scrutinizing the social ramifications of deviance and crime, we pave the way towards fostering a more inclusive and equitable society.

***

Summary

We explored the sociological perspectives on deviance and crime, examining various theoretical frameworks, societal responses, and the role of deviance in social change.

Key Takeaways

- Deviance is a sociocultural appraisal, not an inherent attribute of an action, and can range from benign to criminal.

- Theoretical perspectives on deviance include functionalism (emphasizing social order), conflict theory (highlighting power imbalances), and symbolic interactionism (focusing on social construction).

- Crime is socially constructed, varying across societies and time periods, and influenced by media portrayals.

- Societal responses to deviance range from informal sanctions to formal legal interventions, often exhibiting systemic biases.

- Restorative justice offers an alternative approach to traditional punitive measures.

- Deviance and crime can catalyze social change, challenging power structures, and inspiring reform movements.

- A critical lens is needed to understand the complex interplay between individuals, society, and the construction of deviant or criminal behaviors.

***

QUESTIONS FOR FURTHER THOUGHT

1. Compare and contrast formal and informal deviance, providing examples of each.

2. Explain the functionalist perspective on deviance, and illustrate how it contributes to social order.

3. Describe the conflict perspective on deviance, highlighting the role of power and inequality in shaping definitions

of crime.

4. Summarize the symbolic interactionist perspective on deviance, including the concept of labeling theory and its consequences.

5. Explain how crime is socially constructed, and discuss the influence of the legal system and cultural context on defining criminal acts.

6. Analyze the role of media in shaping public perceptions of crime and its potential impact on marginalized communities.

7. Differentiate between informal and formal societal responses to deviance, providing examples of each and their effectiveness.

8. Describe restorative justice and contrast it with traditional punitive approaches to crime.

9. Discuss how deviance and crime can catalyze social change, providing historical examples.

References For Further Reading

1. Alexander, M. (2010). The New Jim Crow: Mass Incarceration in the Age of Colorblindness.

2. Armstrong, E. (2005). Forging Gay Identities: Organizing Sexuality in San Francisco, 1950-1994.

3. Armstrong, E., & Crage, S. M. (2006). Movements and Memory: The Making of the Stonewall Myth. **American Sociological Review**, 91(5), 524-551.

4. Becker, H. S. (1963). Outsiders: Studies in the Sociology of Deviance.

5. Benson, L. (2013). **Restorative Justice: A Critical Introduction.**

6. Blumer, H. (1969). Symbolic Interactionism: Perspective and Method.

7. Cohen, S. (1972). Folk Devils and Moral Panics: The Creation of the Mods and Rockers.

8. Cohen, A. K. (1955). Delinquent Boys: The Culture of the Gang.

9. Cohen, L. E. (1985). **Theoretical Perspectives in Criminology: An Overview.**

10. Durkheim, É. (1895). The Rules of Sociological Method.

11. Goffman, E. (1963). Stigma: Notes on the Management of Spoiled Identity.

12. Lemert, E. M. (1951). Social Pathology: A Systematic

Approach to the Study of Sociopathic Behavior.

13. Marx, K., & Engels, F. (1848). The Communist Manifesto.

14. Mauer, M. (2006). Race to Incarcerate: A Graphic Retelling.

15. Morris, A. D. (1984). The Origins of the Civil Rights Movement: Black Communities Organizing for Change.

16. Reiner, R. (2007). Law and Order: An Honest Citizen's Guide to Crime and Control.

17. Rock, P. (2007). **Deviance and Control: A Sociological Perspective.**

18. Sutherland, E. H. (1949). Principles of Criminology.

19. Tannenbaum, F. (1938). Crime and the Community.

20. Tilly, C. (2004). Social Movements, 1768–2004.

21. Tonry, M. (1995). Malign Neglect: Race, Crime, and Punishment in America.

22. Zehr, H. (2002). The Little Book of Restorative Justice.

Chapter Eleven

Social Change and Social Movements

Exploring the Intricate Nexus of Social Change and Social Movements

In this chapter, we will navigate the intricate landscape of social change and the dynamics of social movements. By nature, society is an ever-evolving entity, perpetually undergoing transformation (Giddens, 1990). Throughout the annals of history, we have observed social change as a reflexive response to many factors, including technological innovations, economic fluctuations, political revolutions, and cultural shifts (Meyer & Tarrow, 1998). Social movements, conversely, embody the collective endeavors of individuals and groups striving to catalyze meaningful change within society. These movements frequently emerge in reaction to perceived injustices or disparities, aiming to contest prevailing norms, values, and power hierarchies (Tilly, 2004).

Understanding Social Change

Social change encapsulates alterations in social structures, institutions, and behaviors over time (Easterlin, 1996). Manifesting on varying scales—from individual actions to global phenomena—its origins are multifaceted and interwoven, encompassing diverse catalysts such as globalization, urbanization, technological advancement, demographic transitions, environmental shifts, and revolutionary fervor (Castells, 1996).

The ramifications of social change permeate every facet of society, reshaping its economy, politics, cultural paradigms, and social relationships. Such transformations can lead to the advent of new social structures, the attenuation of traditional norms, the reallocation of power, and the redefinition of social identities (Beck, 1992). Analyzing social change equips us with the tools to comprehend the complexities of societal shifts and their extensive implications for individuals and communities alike (Meyer & Tarrow, 1998).

Types of Social Movements

Social movements represent collective initiatives undertaken by groups of individuals unified by a common purpose (Della Porta & Diani, 2006). These movements arise from aspirations for social justice, equality, or the rectification of perceived grievances. They manifest in various forms, each distinguished by its goals, strategies, and target audiences.

Reform Movements

Reform movements seek incremental changes within established social systems and institutions. They aim to rectify specific social issues or injustices while operating within the societal framework (Ginsburg, 1992). Reformers often advocate for policy modifications, pursue legal reforms, and strive to raise public awareness. Their methods may include lobbying, campaigning, and organizing peaceful demonstrations. Prominent examples include the civil rights movement, the women's suffrage movement, labor rights advocacy, and movements advocating for LGBTQ+ rights (Taylor et al., 2008).

Revolutionary Movements

Revolutionary movements aspire to transform existing social and political frameworks fundamentally. These entities seek radical change and frequently challenge prevailing power dynamics (Kriesi, 2004). Their objective is to supplant the established system with an entirely new social order, often employing unconventional tactics such as armed resistance, mass uprisings, and the promotion of revolutionary ideologies. Notable historical instances include the French Revolution, the Russian Revolution, and the contemporary Arab Spring, arising from the inadequacy of reformist efforts and a burgeoning desire for profound transformation (Goodwin, 2001).

Resistance Movements

Resistance movements emerge as a counteraction to oppressive or discriminatory practices enacted by those in power. These movements strive to challenge and subvert the prevailing social order, demanding justice and liberation (Luber, 2015). Often rooted within marginalized or oppressed communities, resistance movements seek to dismantle systems of discrimination and reclaim autonomy through civil disobedience, nonviolent protests, and direct action. Noteworthy examples include the anti-apartheid struggle in South Africa, the American civil rights movement, and ongoing indigenous rights movements worldwide.

Environmental Movements

Environmental movements assert their focus on addressing ecological issues while advocating for sustainable practices (Dunlap & Catton, 1979). These initiatives underscore the intricate connections between social systems and the environment, championing environmental justice, conservation, and mitigation of harmful practices. Activities may include lobbying, awareness-raising campaigns, and direct action to safeguard natural resources and confront climate change. Historical instances range from the environmental movement of the 1960s to the contemporary climate justice campaigns led by activists like Greta Thunberg and various grassroots initiatives aimed at preserving fragile ecosystems (McAdam et al., 2005).

Identity-Based Movements

Identity-based movements concentrate on challenging and altering societal perceptions, norms, and structures related to specific identities (Della Porta & Diani, 2006). They endeavor to confront discrimination and inequality faced by marginalized groups based on race, gender, sexuality, disability, and religion. Their objectives encompass the advocacy for equal rights, enhanced representation, and broader social inclusion. Examples of such movements include Black Lives Matter, feminist movements, disability rights initiatives, and efforts advocating for indigenous rights (Taylor et al., 2008).

Global Justice Movements

Global justice movements address systemic inequalities, exploitation, and oppression transnationally (Cohen, 2004). They emphasize the interconnectedness of global issues while advocating for international solidarity, fair trade practices, and upholding human rights. These movements contest the prevailing global economic structures, promote sustainable development, and advocate for a more equitable distribution of resources. Illustrative examples include the anti-globalization movements, Occupy Wall Street, and campaigns opposing inequitable international trade policies (Steger, 2009).

Social Movements and Their Role in Social Change

Social movements are pivotal in facilitating social change. They serve as platforms for collective action, activism, and the mobilization of individuals united by shared grievances or aspirations (Tilly, 2004). Social movements confront established structures and norms through protests, demonstrations, advocacy efforts, and public awareness campaigns, demanding social justice and transformative change.

The influence of social movements extends to public opinion, cultural norms, policy alterations, and even historical trajectories. They cultivate spaces for dialogue, dissent, and the expression of marginalized voices (Earl, 2007). By challenging the status quo, social movements contribute significantly to societal evolution, advocating for inclusivity, equality, and justice.

Nevertheless, it is imperative to recognize that social change is neither linear nor predictable. Movements often encounter obstacles, setbacks, and resistance from those who benefit from existing power structures (Meyer, 2004). The success or failure of social movements is contingent upon a complex interplay of social, political, economic, and cultural factors. It can vary based on the strategies employed, contextual circumstances, and the level of societal support (Della Porta, 2010).

Conclusion

Social change and social movements are formidable forces shaping the course of human society. They encapsulate the aspirations, struggles, and resilience of individuals and communities striving toward a more equitable world. A deeper comprehension of the underlying causes, manifestations, and effects of social change and social movements enriches our understanding of societal complexities and the transformative power of collective action. These movements epitomize the potential of unified conviction, underscoring the necessity of perpetually challenging and reimagining our social frameworks to foster a just and equitable future.

***

Summary

We explored social change and movements, detailing their types (reform, revolutionary, resistance, environmental, identity-based, and global justice), their roles in societal transformation, and their challenges.

Key Takeaways

- Society constantly evolves and transforms due to various factors, including technological innovations, economic fluctuations, and cultural shifts.

- Social movements are collective endeavors aiming to catalyze meaningful change, often reacting to perceived injustices.

- Different types of social movements exist, each with unique goals and strategies (reform, revolutionary, resistance, environmental, identity-based, and global justice movements).

- Social movements facilitate social change by influencing public opinion, policy, and historical trajectories.

- Social change is complex and not always linear or predictable. It often encounters resistance from those benefiting from existing power structures.

- Understanding social change and social movements is vital for comprehending societal complexities and the power of collective action.

- The success or failure of social movements depends on various factors, including strategies, context, and societal support.

**

QUESTIONS FOR FURTHER THOUGHT

1. Define social change and explain at least three factors that contribute to it, using examples from the text.

2. Describe the difference between reform, revolutionary, resistance, and environmental social movements, providing a real-world example for each.

3. What are the key characteristics of identity-based movements and global justice movements? Give examples of each and explain how they aim to effect change.

4. Explain the concept of social stratification and its connection to social movements. How do social movements challenge social stratification?

5. Discuss the role of social movements in influencing public opinion, policy, and historical trajectories. Provide specific examples from the text.

6. What challenges and obstacles do social movements often face? Explain how the success or failure of a movement depends on various factors.

7. Based on the provided text, explain the relationship between social change and social movements. Are they always intertwined, and if not, how can they differ?

8. Summarize the different types of social movements discussed in the text and analyze their common goals and strategies.

9. How does the text define social structures and institutions, and what is their key difference?

10. Choose one social institution (e.g., family, education, economy, politics) and discuss its functions and how it contributes to both social stability and social change. Use examples from the text and your own knowledge.

References For Further Reading

1. Beck, U. (1992). **Risk Society: Towards a New Modernity.**

2. Castells, M. (1996). **The Information Age: Economy, Society and Culture.**

3. Cohen, M. (2004). **Globalization and Social Movements: Development and Change.**

4. Della Porta, D., & Diani, M. (2006). **Social Movements: An Introduction.**

5. Della Porta, D. (2010). **Methodological Practices in Social Movement Research.**

6. Dunlap, R. E., & Catton, W. R. (1979). **Environmental Sociology.** In: **Research in Social Problems and Public Policy.**

7. Easterlin, R. A. (1996). **Growing Up in America: The Challenge Facing Children in the Twenty-First Century.**

8. Earl, J. (2007). **The Impact of Social Movements on Society.**

9. Giddens, A. (1990). **The Consequences of Modernity.**

10. Ginsburg, F. (1992). **The Politics of Difference: Culture, Representation, and Social Change.**

11. Goodwin, J. (2001). **No Other Way Out: States and**

Revolutionary Movements, 1945-1991.**

12. Kriesi, H. (2004). **Political Contexts and the Impact of Social Movements.**

13. McAdam, D., Tarrow, S. G., & Tilly, C. (2005). **Dynamics of Contention.**

14. Meyer, D. S., & Tarrow, S. (1998). **The Social Movement Society: Contentious Politics for a New Century.**

15. Meyer, D. (2004). **Social Movements in a Time of Social Change.**

16. Steger, M. (2009). **Globalization: A Very Short Introduction.**

17. Taylor, V., Whittier, N., & Morris, A. (2008). **Feminist Frontiers.**

18. Tilly, C. (2004). **Social Movements, 1768–2004.**

Chapter Twelve

The Future of Sociology

The Future of Sociology: Navigating Challenges and Opportunities

As an academic discipline, sociology has traversed significant developments since its establishment, yielding profound insights into human behavior, social constructs, and the intricate web of our globalized existence. As we gaze toward the horizon, it becomes imperative for sociologists and society at large to critically assess the trajectory of sociology. This chapter will elucidate the potential challenges, opportunities, and emergent trends poised to shape the discipline's future (Giddens, 1990).

The Evolving Landscape

The contemporary world is in a state of perpetual evolution, characterized by rapid technological progress, demographic shifts, and transforming societal norms. These phenomena pose both challenges and avenues for growth within sociology. As we advance, sociologists are tasked with adapting their methodologies, theoretical frameworks, and research approaches to effectively capture the complexities of these transformations (Ritzer, 2011). Embracing interdisciplinary collaboration and drawing insights from psychology, economics, biology, and neuroscience is essential for a holistic understanding of the multifaceted social phenomena emerging in this dynamic environment (Baker et al., 1999).

Globalization and Transnationalism

Globalization has indelibly altered societies, dissolving geographic boundaries and fostering unprecedented interconnectedness. The future of sociology will likely center on examining the dynamics of globalization and its repercussions on culture, politics, and social inequality (Sassen, 2007). Sociologists will be called upon to investigate transnational social movements, migration trends, and the evolution of the global labor market, alongside how individuals and communities adapt to these novel global realities (Castells, 2010).

Within globalization, sociologists will focus on the ramifications of economic integration on societal frameworks. They will scrutinize the implications of free trade agreements, the influence of multinational corporations, and the workings of global financial systems on issues such as income inequality, labor rights, and wealth distribution (Piketty, 2014). Additionally, an investigation into the rise of global cities, the formation of transnational identities, and the challenges nation-states face in preserving cultural diversity in the wake of a homogenized global culture will be paramount (Beauregard, 2014).

Technology and Society

Technological advancements are rapidly redefining social interactions, communication practices, and the very fabric of our societies. As sociologists, it is critical to analyze the ramifications of technological innovations on social relationships, privacy, and identity development (Turkle, 2011). The future of sociology will encompass comprehensive studies of Artificial Intelligence, robotics, virtual reality, and the Internet of Things, exploring their roles in shaping social institutions and interactions (West, 2018).

Particularly significant will be the examination of technology's influence on the labor market. Sociologists will investigate the ramifications of automation, including job displacement, income disparity, and the evolving division of labor (Brynjolfsson & McAfee, 2014). Moreover, the implications of digital platforms and the gig economy on workers' rights and the erosion of traditional employment frameworks will warrant thorough scrutiny (De Stefano, 2016). The sociological inquiry will also engage with the ethical ramifications of technological progress, addressing concerns around data privacy, algorithmic bias, and the digital divide (O'Neil, 2016).

Environmental Challenges

The urgent challenge of climate change presents monumental obstacles for societies worldwide, necessitating a sociological inquiry into its social consequences, resource distribution, and environmental justice issues (Gordon & Radcliffe, 2000). The future of sociology will involve analyzing how individuals, communities, and governments respond to ecological crises and how social structures affect our capacity for sustainable solutions.

Sociologists will explore the intersectionality of social factors and environmental challenges, investigating how race, class, and gender shape vulnerability to climate change and access to critical resources (Bullard, 2000). They will also consider the social repercussions of environmental disasters and the grassroots movements that respond to such crises. A pivotal part of sociological research will involve understanding and addressing the social dimensions of sustainability, including ecologically responsible consumption, innovative urban planning, and transitions to renewable energy sources (Fischer, 2019).

Social Justice and Inequality

Sociology must continue to confront issues of social justice and inequality in an age marked by persistent social inequities. The discipline's future will involve an increased focus on research and advocacy directed at dismantling systemic discrimination, addressing economic disparities, and investigating the impact of globalization on marginalized communities (Crenshaw, 1991). Sociologists will strive to uncover and challenge the social structures that perpetuate inequality, including systemic racism, sexism, classism, and homophobia (Wilkins, 2015).

Adopting intersectional frameworks to study inequality will become essential, acknowledging that categories such as race, gender, sexuality, and disability intertwine, compounding the experiences and outcomes of individuals in society (Collins, 2000). Sociologists will examine how power dynamics operate within these intersecting structures, shedding light on how multiple forms of privilege and oppression shape societal hierarchies. Furthermore, innovative methodologies, such as participatory research and community-based interventions, will be employed to promote social justice alongside policy advocacy (Minkler & Wallerstein, 2003).

Conclusion

As sociology looks ahead, its relevance and capacity to influence society remain critical. The discipline must continually adapt to the shifting landscape, embracing new methodologies, theoretical frameworks, and interdisciplinary partnerships. Sociologists will be positioned to play a pivotal role in fostering a more equitable and sustainable future by focusing on emergent trends in globalization, technology, environmental issues, and social justice.

The future of sociology rests in its adeptness at providing incisive insights, informing policy frameworks, and positively contributing to societal advancement. Through rigorous research, active engagement with diverse communities, and a steadfast commitment to social justice, sociology will evolve and remain an indispensable instrument for understanding and transforming our intricate social world.

***

Summary

We explored the future of sociology, focusing on challenges and opportunities presented by globalization, technological advancements, environmental concerns, and social justice issues, emphasizing the need for interdisciplinary collaboration and adaptable methodologies.

Key Takeaways

- The future of sociology requires adapting methodologies to address rapid technological progress, demographic shifts, and evolving societal norms.
- Globalization's impact on culture, politics, social in-

equality, and transnational social movements will be a key focus.

- The influence of technology on social interactions, labor markets, and ethical considerations (AI, automation, data privacy) needs to be thoroughly investigated.

- Climate change's social consequences, resource distribution, and environmental justice issues demand sociological analysis.

- Addressing persistent social inequalities, systemic discrimination, and marginalized communities will remain central.

- Intersectional frameworks will be crucial for understanding how race, gender, and other factors compound inequality.

- Sociology's future depends on insightful research, community engagement, and commitment to social justice for societal advancement.

***

QUESTIONS FOR FURTHER THOUGHT

1. According to the text, what are three major challenges facing sociology in the future?

2. How does globalization impact the future direction of sociological research, and what specific areas will sociologists focus on?

3. Explain how technological advancements, specifically artificial intelligence and automation, are expected to shape sociological inquiry.

4. Discuss the role of sociology in addressing climate change and environmental justice issues, including the intersectionality of these issues with other social factors.

5. How will sociology address social justice and inequality in the future, and what methodologies might be employed?

6. What is the significance of interdisciplinary collaboration in shaping the future of sociology? Provide examples of relevant disciplines.

7. Explain the evolving landscape of sociology and the need for adapting methodologies and theoretical frameworks.

8. How will sociologists analyze the impact of economic integration and globalization on income inequality and wealth distribution?

9. Define the concept of intersectionality in the context of studying inequality and discuss its relevance for future sociological research.

10. What is the overall conclusion regarding sociology's future relevance and role in shaping a more equitable and sustainable future?

References For Further Reading

- Baker, M., Jones, R. W., & Garcia, E. (1999). *Interdisciplinary Perspectives on Human Behavior*. New York: Academic Press.

- Beauregard, R. A. (2014). *Global Cities: A Social and Political Perspective*. Urban Affairs Review, 50(4), 478-481.

- Brynjolfsson, E., & McAfee, A. (2014). *The Second Machine Age: Work, Progress, and Prosperity in a Time of Brilliant Technologies*. New York: W. W. Norton & Company.

- Bullard, R.D. (2000). *Dumping in Dixie: Race, Class, and Environmental Quality*. Boulder, CO: Westview Press.

- Castells, M. (2010). *The Rise of the Network Society*. Malden, MA: Blackwell Publishing.

- Collins, P.H. (2000). *Black Feminist Thought: Knowledge, Consciousness, and the Politics of Empowerment*. New York: Routledge.

- Crenshaw, K. (1991). Mapping the Margins: Intersectionality, Identity Politics, and Violence against Women of Color. *Stanford Law Review*, 43(6), 1241-1299.

- De Stefano, V. (2016). *The Rise of the "Just-in-Time" Workforce: On-Demand Work, Crowd Work, and Labor Protection in the Gig Economy*. Comparative Labor Law & Policy Journal, 37(3), 471-503.

- Fischer, F. (2019). *Sustainability: A Systems and Multi-*

disciplinary Perspective. New York: Routledge.

- Giddens, A. (1990). *The Consequences of Modernity.* Stanford University Press.

- Gordon, D. & Radcliffe, B. (2000). *Environmental Policy and Justice.* Urban Affairs Review, 35(6), 784-800.

- Minkler, M. & Wallerstein, N. (2003). *Community-Based Participatory Research for Health.* San Francisco, CA: Jossey-Bass.

- O'Neil, C. (2016). *Weapons of Math Destruction: How Big Data Increases Inequality and Threatens Democracy.* New York: Crown Publishing.

- Piketty, T. (2014). *Capital in the Twenty-First Century.* Cambridge, MA: Harvard University Press.

- Ritzer, G. (2011). *Sociological Theory.* New York: McGraw-Hill.

- Sassen, S. (2007). *A Sociology of Globalization.* New York: W. W. Norton & Company.

- Turkle, S. (2011). *Alone Together: Why We Expect More from Technology and Less from Each Other.* New York: Basic Books.

- West, D. M. (2018). *The Future of Work: Robots, AI, and Automation.* Washington, D.C.: Brookings Institution Press.

- Wilkins, R. (2015). *Race, Class, and Social Capital: The Intersections of Inequality.* Sociology Compass, 9(11), 931-943.

Chapter Thirteen

Conclusion: A Reflective Journey Through Sociology

In this final chapter, we reflect on the insightful exploration of sociology presented throughout this book. This contemplative step encourages us to consider the rich ideas and themes we've encountered along the way. We have delved deeply into the complex social fabric that weaves our lives together, unraveling its intricacies and multifaceted nature. In this space of introspection, we pause to meticulously examine the key insights and perspectives that have emerged from our immersive exploration.

As we reflect on the preceding chapters, we find solace in recognizing the profound interconnections that bind society. From the foundational principles of sociology to contemporary postmodern paradigms, we have witnessed the continuously evolving tapestry of social existence. Theoretical frameworks such as functionalism, conflict theory, symbolic interactionism, and feminist theory have illuminated our understanding, offering diverse lenses through which we scrutinize the social landscape. These frameworks serve as invaluable intellectual tools, guiding our analysis and enabling us to decipher the intricate webs of social interactions and the processes of meaning-making. Yet, amid our rigorous inquiry, we acknowledge the limitations inherent in our interpretations, recognizing that the complexity of society remains elusive and ever-changing.

Our exploration has unveiled that the critical processes of socialization and identity formation are at the heart of human existence. We have probed into the essence of humanity itself, examining how individuals absorb norms, values, and beliefs that shape their thoughts, behaviors, and overall sense of self. From the influences of family dynamics to educational institutions and the pervasive effects of media and peer networks, layers of socialization envelop each individual, intricately shaping our very beings. Through this lens, we have come to appreciate the delicate interplay between agency and structure, understanding that while individuals exert influence on society, they are simultaneously shaped by it.

Within the socio-structural context, we have immersed ourselves in the complex web of social relations and institutions that govern our lives. Our analyses have meticulously dissected the systems of power and domination that perpetuate social stratification and inequality. From class distinctions to discrimination based on race, gender, sexuality, and other social categories, we have investigated the intricate mechanisms that maintain unequal access to resources and opportunities. Our examination of capitalism, patriarchy, racism, and other forms of oppression has illuminated the myriad ways that privilege and disadvantage are entrenched within the social fabric, reminding us of the ongoing struggles for justice and equality.

Yet, amidst this backdrop of inequity, we have also celebrated the rich tapestry of cultural diversity. As cultural anthropologists within the sociological field, we have developed a profound appreciation for the significance of culture and its impact on human behavior and societal norms. We have explored the complexity of symbols, rituals, and worldviews that comprise our cultural milieu. From language and art to religion and cuisine, culture fundamentally shapes our identities and lends meaning to our existence. It operates as a dynamic force, constantly evolving in response to the shifting social landscape. Through the lens of multiculturalism, we have recognized the imperative of valuing diverse cultural perspectives and fostering inclusivity, thereby challenging dominant narratives that marginalize certain groups.

Our deliberations have led us to confront the challenging concepts of deviance and crime as we ventured into society's darker corners. We have critically examined the social construction of these concepts, acknowledging that normative boundaries are not rigid but rather socially negotiated and portrayed. The dynamics of power and control underpinning these constructions have been revealed, showcasing the layers of societal reactions and their varied impacts on individuals. We have fostered a more nuanced understanding of deviance, questioning the foundations of what is deemed "normal." Additionally, we have explored the social institutions of punishment and rehabilitation, uncovering how the criminal justice system perpetuates inequality and further marginalizes specific communities.

Finally, we have engaged with the fields of social change and social movements, identifying the forces that drive societies forward or anchor them in inertia. Through a sociological lens, we have examined the catalysts for social transformation, delving into the mechanisms of resistance and collective action that challenge and reshape social order. From grassroots movements to revolutions, the rise and fall of ideologies, and the transformative power of social media, social change emerges as an intricate dance between agency and structure, individual action, and collective will. We have grappled with the complexities of various social movements, differentiating their strategies—from reformist approaches seeking gradual change to radical efforts demanding fundamental societal transformations. Furthermore, we have scrutinized the influences of technology and globalization on social change, appreciating the interplay between local dynamics and global currents.

As we draw the curtain on this book, we must recognize that sociology is not merely an intellectual exercise but a potent instrument for societal transformation. By unraveling the social forces that shape our lives, we bear the substantial responsibility to actively engage in crafting a more inclusive and equitable world. We must reject the role of passive observers and actively embrace our positions as agents of change. This challenge calls for understanding and analyzing our world and taking concrete, informed actions to elevate marginalized voices and challenge injustice.

Our concluding reflections remind us that this exploration has merely skimmed the surface of sociology's vast depth. The expanse of the social realm remains tantalizingly elusive, urging us to persist in seeking understanding, questioning assumptions, and challenging the status quo. As society continues its evolution, so must our sociological imagination and engagement. We hope that this excursion into sociology ignites a passionate desire within you to continue uncovering society's hidden intricacies, empowering you to contribute intentionally and compassionately to our collective human experience.

May your sociological journey be an enduring pursuit, inspiring you to embark on a lifelong quest for knowledge, social awareness, and transformation.

References For Further Reading

1. Alexander, M. (2010). *The New Jim Crow: Mass Incarceration in the Age of Colorblindness.* New Press.

2. Appadurai, A. (1996). *Modernity at Large: Cultural Dimensions of Globalization.* University of Minnesota Press.

3. Becker, H. S. (1963). *Outsiders: Studies in the Sociology of Deviance.* Free Press.

4. Berger, P. L., & Luckmann, T. (1967). *The Social Construction of Reality: A Treatise in the Sociology of Knowledge.* Anchor Books.

5. Beck, U. (1992). *Risk Society: Towards a New Modernity.* Sage Publications.

6. Bourdieu, P. (1986). *The Forms of Capital.* In *Handbook of Theory and Research for the Sociology of Education* (pp. 241-258). Greenwood.

7. Castells, M. (2012). *Networks of Outrage and Hope: Social Movements in the Internet Age.* Polity Press.

8. Crenshaw, K. (1989). Demarginalizing the Intersection of Race and Sex: A Black Feminist Critique of Antidiscrimination Doctrine, Feminist Theory and Antiracist Politics. *University of Chicago Legal Forum*, 1989(1), 139-167.

9. Della Porta, D., & Diani, M. (2006). *Social Movements: An Introduction.* Blackwell Publishing.

10. Geertz, C. (1973). *The Interpretation of Cultures: Selected*

Essays. Basic Books.

11. Giddens, A. (1990). *The Consequences of Modernity*. Stanford University Press.

12. Harrison, L. E. (2008). *Culture Matters: How Values Shape Human Progress*. Basic Books.

13. Haraway, D. J. (1988). *Situated Knowledges: The Science Studies Reader*. Routledge.

14. Hofstede, G. (2001). *Culture's Consequences: Comparing Values, Behaviors, Institutions, and Organizations Across Nations*. Sage Publications.

15. Lemert, E. M. (1951). *Social Pathology: A Systematic Approach to the Study of Society*. McGraw-Hill.

16. Macionis, J. J., & Plummer, K. (2012). *Sociology*. Pearson.

17. Marx, K. (1867). *Capital: Critique of Political Economy*. Penguin Classics.

18. Ritzer, G. (2011). *Sociological Theory*. McGraw-Hill.

19. Tilly, C., & Tarrow, S. (2015). *Contentious performances*. Cambridge University Press.

20. Wallerstein, I. (1991). *The Modern World System: Capitalist Agriculture and the Origins of the European World-Economy in the Sixteenth Century*. University of California Press.

Chapter Fourteen

Sources and References

Note to the French readers:

For all the references and sources we cited, and much more in French, please consult *"Les Classiques des sciences sociales"* de l'université du Québec à Montréal. All the books are available in French for free download. Here is the link: https://classiques.uqam.ca/

Alexander, M. (2010). *The new Jim Crow: Mass incarceration in the age of colorblindness*. New Press.

Appadurai, A. (1996). *Modernity at large: Cultural dimensions of globalization*. University of Minnesota Press.

Babbie, E. (2021). *The basics of social research* (7th ed.). Cengage Learning.

Baumeister, R. F. (1998). The self. In D. T. Gilbert, S. T. Fiske, & G. Lindzey (Eds.), *The Handbook of* Social Psychology (Vol. 1, pp. 680-740). McGraw-Hill.

Becker, G. S. (1962). Irrational behavior in economic theory.

Southern Economic Journal, 29(2), 113-122.

Becker, H. S. (1963). *Outsiders: Studies in the sociology of deviance.* Free Press.

Beauchamp, T. L., & Childress, J. F. (2013). *Principles of biomedical ethics* (7th ed.). Oxford University Press.

Beck, U. (1992). *Risk society: Towards a new modernity.* Sage Publications.

Bengtson, V. L. (2001). Beyond the nuclear family: The increasing importance of extended family in American society. In V. L. Bengtson, P. N. Antonucci, & J. B. B. Silverstein (Eds.), *Handbook of theories of aging* (pp. 535-552). Springer.

Berger, P. L., & Luckmann, T. (1966). *The social construction of reality: A treatise in the sociology of knowledge.* Anchor Books.

Berger, P. L., & Luckmann, T. (1967). *The social construction of reality: A treatise in sociology of knowledge.* Anchor Books.

Berman, S. (2013). *Civil society and the emergence of the modern state.* The University of Chicago Press.

Bourguignon, F. (2015). The globalization of the inequality: Theoretical and methodological issues. In *Measuring global inequality* (pp. 5-34). Palgrave Macmillan.

Bourdieu, P. (1984). *Distinction: A social critique of the judgment of taste.* Harvard University Press.

Bourdieu, P. (1986). The forms of capital. In J. G. Richardson (Ed.), *Handbook of theory and research for the sociology of education* (pp. 241-258). Greenwood Press.

Bowles, S., & Gintis, H. (1976). *Schooling in capitalist America.* Basic Books.

Bronfenbrenner, U. (1979). *The ecology of human development: Experiments by nature and design*. Harvard University Press.

Bryman, A. (2016). *Social research methods* (5th ed.). Oxford University Press.

Brynjolfsson, E., & McAfee, A. (2014). *The second machine age: Work, progress, and prosperity in a time of brilliant technologies*. W. W. Norton & Company.

Burgess, R. G. (1988). *Keeping research: A guide to the sociology of religion*. Wiley.

Cascio, E. U., & Schanzenbach, D. W. (2013). The effect of school quality on students' long-term earnings: Evidence from a randomized experiment. *Review of Economics and Statistics, 95*(3), 911-927.

Castells, M. (1996). *The information age: Economy, society and culture*. Blackwell Publishing.

Castells, M. (2010). *The rise of the network society* (2nd ed.). Wiley-Blackwell.

Castells, M. (2012). *Networks of outrage and hope: Social movements in the internet age*. Polity Press.

Chaves, M. (2011). The future of American religious diversity. *The Forum, 9*(1), Article 5.

Cohen, A. K. (1955). *Delinquent boys: The culture of the gang*. Free Press.

Cohen, L. E. (1985). Theoretical perspectives in criminology: An overview. *Theoretical Criminology, 1*(2), 203-221.

Cohen, S. (1972). *Folk devils and moral panics: The creation of the mods and rockers*. MacGibbon & Kee.

Collins, P. H. (1990). *Black feminist thought: Knowledge, consciousness, and the politics of empowerment.* Routledge.

Collins, P. H. (2000). *Black feminist thought: Knowledge, consciousness, and the politics of empowerment.* Routledge.

Comte, A. (1830). *Course in positive philosophy.* http://www.gutenberg.org/files/37717/37717-h/37717-h.htm

Cook, T. D., & Campbell, D. T. (1979). *Quasi-experimentation: Design & analysis issues for field settings.* Houghton Mifflin.

Crenshaw, K. (1989). Demarginalizing the intersection of race and sex: A black feminist critique of antidiscrimination doctrine, feminist theory and antiracist politics. *University of Chicago Legal Forum, 1989*(1), 139-167.

Dahrendorf, R. (1959). *Class and class conflict in industrial society.* Stanford University Press.

Della Porta, D., & Diani, M. (2006). *Social movements: An introduction.* Blackwell Publishing.

DeWalt, K. M., & DeWalt, B. R. (2010). *Participant observation: A guide for researchers.* Rowman & Littlefield.

Denzin, N. K., & Lincoln, Y. S. (2011). *The SAGE Handbook of qualitative research* (4th ed.). SAGE Publications.

Duncan, O. D., & Puma, J. C. (2016). The measurement of social inequality. In R. K. Merton (Ed.), *On social inequality: A historical perspective* (pp. 15-40). Transaction Publishers.

Durkheim, É. (1893). *The division of labor in society.* Free Press.

Durkheim, É. (1895). *The rules of sociological method.* Free Press.

Durkheim, É. (1897). *Suicide: A study in sociology.* Free Press.

Eagleton, T. (2011). *Why Marx was right.* Yale University Press.

Elias, N. (2000). *The civilizing process.* Blackwell.

Ewick, P., & Silbey, S. S. (1995). Entwined empires: The impact of American and English law on society. *Law and Society Review, 29*(4), 1057-1076.

Fischer, F. (2019). *Sustainability: A systems and multidisciplinary perspective.* Routledge.

Flick, U. (2018). *An introduction to qualitative research* (6th ed.). SAGE Publications.

Freud, S. (1920). *Beyond the pleasure principle.* http://www.gutenberg.org/files/49417/49417-h/49417-h.htm

Furstenberg, F. F. (2000). The sociology of adolescent development. In W. Damon & R. M. Lerner (Eds.), *Handbook of child psychology* (Vol. 1, pp. 95-139). John Wiley & Sons, Inc.

Furstenberg, F. F. (2000). The unplanned revolution: Changing families in a changing world. In D. P. Moynihan (Ed.), *Social democracy and the family* (pp. 50-66). W. W. Norton.

Giddens, A. (1984). *The constitution of society: Outline of the theory of structuration.* University of California Press.

Giddens, A. (1990). *The consequences of modernity.* Stanford University Press.

Giddens, A. (2000). *Runaway world.* Routledge.

Giddens, A. (2013). *Sociology* (7th ed.). Polity Press.

Giddens, A. (2017). *Sociology* (8th ed.). Polity Press.

Giddens, A., Duneier, M., Appelbaum, R. P., & Carr, D. (2017). *Introduction to* Sociology (10th ed.). W.W. Norton.

Goffman, E. (1959). *The presentation of self in everyday life*. Anchor Books.

Goffman, E. (1963). *Stigma: Notes on the management of spoiled identity*. Prentice Hall.

Goodwin, J. (2001). No other way out: States and revolutionary movements, 1945-1991. *Cambridge University Press*.

Granovetter, M. (1973). The strength of weak ties. *American Journal of Sociology*, 78(6), 1360-1380.

Guetterman, T. C., Fetters, M. D., & Creswell, J. W. (2015). Integrating qualitative and quantitative methods in social research. *SAGE Research Methods*.

Hall, S. (1997). Representation: Cultural representations and signifying practices. In S. Hall (Ed.), *Representation: Cultural representations and signifying practices* (pp. 1-12). SAGE Publications Ltd.

Hannerz, U. (1990). Flows and contradictions in a global setting. In M. Featherstone (Ed.), *Global culture: Nationalism, globalization and modernity* (pp. 38-56). Sage Publications.

Hannerz, U. (1993). Cultural complexity: Studies in the social organization of meaning. *Columbia University Press*.

Haraway, D. J. (1988). Situated knowledges: The science studies reader. *Routledge*.

Henslin, J. M. (2013). *Sociology: A down-to-earth approach* (10th ed.). Pearson Education.

Hofstede, G. (2001). *Culture's consequences: Comparing values, behaviors, institutions, and organizations across nations*. Sage Publications.

Houtman, D., & Aupers, S. (2007). The spiritual turn and the decline of tradition: The spread of postmodern spirituality in contemporary Western society. *Journal of Contemporary Religion*, *22*(2), 203-222.

Hourani, G. F. (1983). Arab seafarers: Ibn Khaldun's interpretation of the evidence. *International Journal of Middle East Studies*, *15*(2), 159-176.

Inglehart, R., & Welzel, C. (2005). *Modernization, cultural change, and democracy: The human development sequence*. Cambridge University Press.

Johnson, R. B., & Onwuegbuzie, A. J. (2004). Mixed methods research: A research paradigm whose time has come. *Educational Researcher*, *33*(7), 14-26.

Kendall, D. (2015). *Sociology in our times* (10th ed.). Cengage Learning.

King, G., Keohane, R. O., & Verba, S. (1994). *Designing social inquiry: Scientific inference in qualitative research*. Princeton University Press.

Kroeber, A. L., & Kluckhohn, C. (1952). Culture: A critical review of concepts and definitions. *American Anthropologist*, *55*(4), 1-42.

Kvale, S., & Brinkmann, S. (2015). *Interviews: Learning the craft of qualitative research interviewing* (3rd ed.). SAGE Publications.

Lasswell, H. D. (1950). *Politics: Who gets what, when, how*. Whittlesey House.

Legewie, J., & DiPrete, T. A. (2012). School context and social stratification: An empirical assessment. *Sociological Science*, *3*, 221-242.

Lemert, E. M. (1951). *Social pathology: A systematic approach to the study of sociopathic behavior*. McGraw-Hill.

Levy, R. I., & Hollan, D. (2001). Person-centered interviewing. In U. Hannerz & M. Featherstone (Eds.), *Global culture: Nationalism, globalization and modernity* (pp. 160-180). Sage Publications.

Lucas, S. R. (2001). Effectively maintained inequality: Educational inequality, status, and social capital. *American Journal of Sociology*, *106*(2), 332-362.

Liamputtong, P. (2007). *Researching the vulnerable: A guide to sensitive research methods*. SAGE Publications.

Mahoney, J., & Thelen, K. (2015). Advances in comparative-historical analysis. *American Political Science Review*, *109*(1), 27-40.

Mair, P. (2006). *Ruling the void: The hollowing of Western democracy*. Verso.

Marx, K. (1867). *Capital: Critique of political economy*. Penguin Classics.

Marx, K., & Engels, F. (1848). *The communist manifesto*. Penguin Classics.

McAdam, D., Tarrow, S., & Tilly, C. (2005). *Dynamics of contention*. Cambridge University Press.

Mason, J. (2018). *Qualitative researching* (3rd ed.). SAGE Publications.

Maucione, M. (2013). An exploration of the relationship between body image and self-esteem. *Canadian Review of Sociology*, *50*(4), 442-464.

Mau, S., & Rüb, F. (2009). *Changing classes: The political orienta-

tion of the great transformation. Rowman & Littlefield.

Mead, G. H. (1934). *Mind, self, and society: From the standpoint of a social behaviorist.* University of Chicago Press.

Messner, M. A. (2000). "Barbie girls vs. sea monsters": Children constructing gender. *Sociological Forum, 15*(2), 221-233.

Mills, C. W. (1956). *The power elite.* Oxford University Press.

Mills, C. W. (1959). *The sociological imagination.* Oxford University Press.

Murdock, G. P. (1945). The common denominator of cultures. *American Anthropologist, 47*(1), 43-57.

Neuendorf, K. A. (2017). *The content analysis guidebook.* SAGE Publications.

Nisbet, R. A. (1969). *The sociological tradition.* Basic Books.

O'Neil, C. (2016). *Weapons of math destruction: How big data increases inequality and threatens democracy.* Crown Publishing.

Papalia, D. E., & Martorell, G. (2015). *Experience human development* (14th ed.). McGraw-Hill.

Patton, M. Q. (2015). *Qualitative research & evaluation methods* (4th ed.). SAGE Publications.

Peters, M. A., & F., M. S. (2014). *Globalization, education, and social justice: A respect for diversity* (2nd ed.). Routledge.

Piketty, T. (2014). *Capital in the twenty-first century.* Belknap Press.

Przeworski, A., & Teune, H. (1970). *Quantitative methodology in comparative politics.* Random House.

Ragin, C. C., & Amato, F. (1994). *Constructing social research: The unity and diversity of method*. Pine Forge Press.

Reskin, B. F. (2012). The race discrimination system. *American Sociological Review, 77*(4), 695-718.

Robson, C., & McCartan, K. (2016). *Real-world research* (4th ed.). Wiley.

Rocco, T. S., Bliss, L., Gallagher, D. J., & Perez-Prado, A. (2003). Taking the next step: Mixed methods research in organizational systems. *Information Technology, Learning, and Performance Journal, 21*(1), 19-26.

Ruggiero, V. (2018). *Sociology: Theory, structure, and action*. New York: Cambridge University Press.

Salkind, N. J. (2010). *Encyclopedia of research design*. SAGE Publications.

Sapir, E. (1921). *Language: An introduction to the study of speech*. Harcourt, Brace and Company.

Scott, J. (1990). *A matter of record: Documentary sources in social research*. Temple University Press.

Scott, W. R. (1995). *Organizations: Rational, natural, and open systems* (3rd ed.). Prentice Hall.

Shadish, W. R., Cook, T. D., & Campbell, D. T. (2002). *Experimental and quasi-experimental designs for generalized causal inference*. Houghton Mifflin.

Silverman, D. (2016). *Doing qualitative research* (4th ed.). SAGE Publications.

Simmel, G. (1971). *On individuality and social forms*. University of Chicago Press.

Sitting Bull, (1999). *The autobiography of Sitting Bull*. In Walter H. and John F. (Eds.), *The American Indian Experience: A History* (pp. 130-137). New York: Wiley.

Steger, M. (2009). *Globalization: A very short introduction*. Oxford University Press.

Stiglitz, J. E. (2012). *The price of inequality: How today's divided society endangers our future*. W.W. Norton & Company.

Swatos, W. H., & Christiano, K. J. (1999). Secularization theory: Measurement and explanation. In W. H. Swatos & K. J. Christiano (Eds.), *Secularization, rationality, and modernity* (pp. 1-20). AltaMira Press.

Tanenbaum, F. (1938). *Crime and the community*. New York: New York University Press.

Tashakkori, A., & Teddlie, C. (2010). *Mixed methodology: Combining qualitative and quantitative approaches*. SAGE Publications.

Taylor, V., Whittier, N., & Morris, A. (2008). *Feminist frontiers* (4th ed.). McGraw-Hill.

Thompson, J. B. (1995). *The media and modernity: A social theory of the media*. Stanford University Press.

Thompson, M. (2012). Social status and health: Evidence from the national longitudinal health survey. *Sociology of Health & Illness*, *34*(8), 1241-1260.

Tilly, C. (2004). *Social movements, 1768–2004*. Paradigm Publishers.

Tilly, C., & Tarrow, S. (2015). *Contentious performances*. Cambridge University Press.

Turkle, S. (2011). *Alone together: Why we expect more from technology and less from each other*. Basic Books.

van der Meer, T. (2009). The study of the historical foundations of religion. *Science and Society, 75*(4), 56-67.

Wacquant, L. (2004). *Body and soul: Notebooks of an apprentice boxer*. Oxford University Press.

Weber, M. (1904). *The Protestant ethic and the spirit of capitalism*. Scribner.

Weber, M. (1922). *Economy and society: An outline of interpretive sociology*. University of California Press.

Weber, M. (1978). *Economy and Society: An Outline of Interpretive Sociology*. University of California Press.

Wilkinson, R., & Pickett, K. (2009). *The spirit level: Why equality is better for everyone*. Penguin.

Wilkinson, R., & Pickett, K. (2010). *The spirit level: Why more equal societies almost always do better*. Allen Lane.

Wimmer, A., & Gallo, J. (2013). A guide to comparative research. *Social Forces, 91*(3), 775-802.

Yeung, H. W. C. (2009). East Asian urbanism: Towards a conceptualization. In T. B. K. Wong & P. W. K. Wong (Eds.), *Urbanizing Asian: Insights from East Asia* (pp. 143-171). Routledge.

Yin, R. K. (2018). *Case study research and applications: Design and methods* (6th ed.). SAGE Publications.

Zimbardo, P. G. (2007). *The Lucifer effect: Understanding how good people turn evil*. Random House.